# 1,001
# BROADWAYS

*Hometown Talent*
*on Stage*

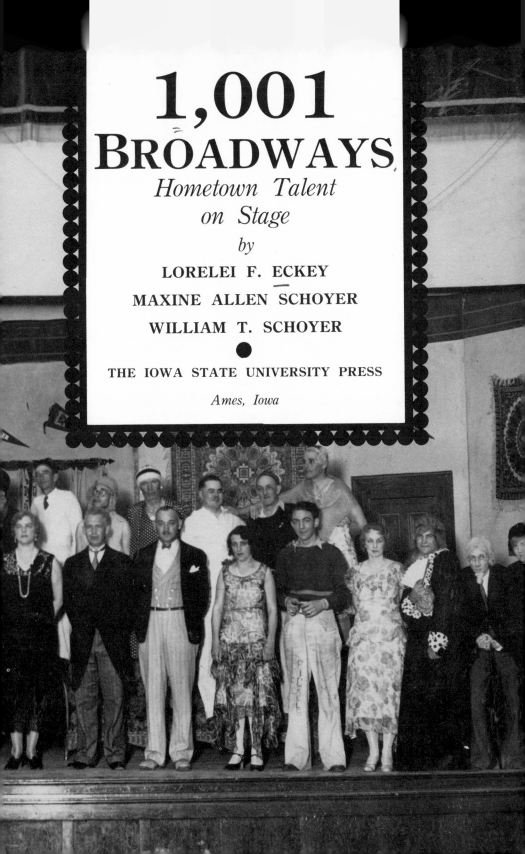

# 1,001
# BROADWAYS,
*Hometown Talent
on Stage*

*by*

## LORELEI F. ECKEY

## MAXINE ALLEN SCHOYER

## WILLIAM T. SCHOYER

●

**THE IOWA STATE UNIVERSITY PRESS**

*Ames, Iowa*

FRONTISPIECE: A stylish *Aunt Lucia* cast at Brawley, Calif.

PAGE 1: Franceswayne Allen during her peak years as one of the nation's foremost home talent playwrights and directors.

PAGE 2: Childhood portrait suggests the irrepressible energy that often led Fran Allen into trouble.

PN
3161
E3
1982

**Library of Congress Cataloging in Publication Data**

Eckey, Lorelei F.
  1,001 Broadways.

  Bibliography: p.
  Includes index.
  1. Amateur theater—United States—History—20th century. 2. Allen, Franceswayne. 3. Universal Producing Company. 4. Acting teachers—United States—Biography. I. Schoyer, Maxine, 1910–    II. Schoyer, William T., 1908–    III. Title. IV. Title: One thousand and one Broadways.
PN3161.E3    1982      792'.0222'0973      82–14806
**ISBN 0–8138–1284–4**

# CONTENTS

# FOREWORD

*I well remember* the dramatic coaches of home talent shows in which I performed as a child. Usually we called them "the mean old coaches" because of how they ordered us around. A picture comes back to me of the coach who taught us the Russian Cossack dance.

"Down, down, down!" she would shout at us. "Get your bottoms almost to the floor but don't lose your balance. Cross your forearms before your chest like this. Now kick each leg out one at a time. One, two; one, two! Don't lose your balance, don't fall!"

My friend Bubble and I had a hard time mastering this Russian dance, but we were challenging each other to be the star in the junior part of a home talent show, *The Follies of 1920.* We were in the cast putting it on for our fathers, who were Elks and depending on us to help raise money. My sister Franceswayne Allen, the subject of this book, was highly critical of our efforts. "You'll probably tip over and crack your stupid head," she said cheerfully.

Franceswayne, four years older, was in the Maidens Chorus. She and her high school friends were making merry with their acts of doing the Charleston and dramatic parts. They seemed to think they ought to have their names in lights over the Columbia Theater on Broadway in our hometown, Columbia, Mo.

All the nine- to twelve-year-olds, like Bubble and me, were in the second scene of the show. At least we could look down on the opening act called the Baby Pageant. They hadn't anything to do but sway back and forth while a storytelling lady sang "Take Me Back to Babyland." Bubble and I felt we were the feature of the show once we could dance like Cossacks. If we had been older we could have been the romantic leads in the play that followed, but for that you had to have a boyfriend who could act in the cast opposite you.

After our act came the Maidens Chorus and then the Flapper Chorus made of grown-up men like my father and the other Elks. All they did was dress in women's clothes and act silly and get a lot of laughs. Then Franceswayne returned as an ingenue in the play. But our time would come, because next year maybe another organization such as my mother's United Daughters of the Confederacy would put on a new show, maybe from another producing company. Every year you looked forward to when a home talent show was booked into your town and you were a part of it. It was exciting when you heard the applause.

All of us grade school Russian Cossacks hated and rebelled against the mean old dramatic coach. Never mind that she made you perform at a level you never reached in amateur dramatics before or perhaps since. Never mind that back of the applause were her whip-cracking demands for you to do the routine over and over until you were giving your best. That was something you would perhaps realize and appreciate years afterward. At the time we had to report to her for rehearsal right after school every afternoon until supper time, and work, work, work. She never let you have any fun. She yelled at you if you let down. Why was she so strict? Why did she have to be such a bully? But Mother said we must obey her because the BPOE needed the money.

Franceswayne and her group, because they were in acts with boys, seemed to like rehearsing. Franceswayne liked it better than anyone, even to the point of admiring our mean old coach. She seemed to think that being a dramatic coach was the greatest career a girl could have. She had been bitten by the show business bug and never got over it. That's what this book is about.

*Maxine Allen Schoyer*

# PREFACE

*This book was written* to tell the story of small-town show business and the home talent shows it produced. Many millions of Americans viewed these productions, probably more than attended all the Broadway plays of the period. Perhaps as many as a million persons performed in them as amateur actors. Yet heretofore nothing substantial has been written about this type of theater which, for nearly three-quarters of a century, provided community amusement in villages and medium-size towns.

We have told this story, not through a ponderous history, but rather by recounting the lively saga of one producing firm and its premiere dramatic coach–playwright over an eight-year period during the heyday of home talent shows. The company was the Universal Producing Company of Fairfield, Iowa, the leader in its field from 1928 to 1935. The coach, Franceswayne Allen of Columbia, Mo., seemed born for this branch of show biz.

The accomplishments and trials of Universal and its dynamic owners—brothers Raymond, Wilson, Merle, and Weston Stewart—and of Fran Allen, largely reflect those of the industry as a whole. At the same time our subjects represent the industry at its best in terms of successful innovation and contribution to the entertainment scene. We feel they illustrate what hometown show business meant to America.

Home talent shows took the form of plays, musicals, minstrels, pageants, revues, or combinations of these, written or adapted by a professional producing company. The company contracted with a sponsoring civic organization to produce the show in its town, using local citizens as actors, hence the term home talent. Profits were split with the sponsor. The company supplied a professional director to recruit and direct the cast, do the promotion, and get the tickets sold. Also supplied were scripts, costumes, and sometimes scenery.

Home talent productions were popular because they offered everyone so inclined an opportunity to act in a theatrical production and all others the spectacle of friends and local dignitaries performing in roles from musical to amusing. The casts made extensive use of children and young people, swelling the audiences with proud parents and relatives. Financially, the shows provided a small monetary windfall to the sponsor. Since the receipts usually were earmarked for a local charity or other worthy cause, the performances were welcomed by the community.

Home talent shows flourished from the late 1800s, when the completion of rail networks opened easy access for show bookers and directors to midwestern small towns, to the 1960s, when TV preempted community entertainment. One of the first such shows recorded was a children's operetta, *The Brownies in Fairyland,* about the characters in a comic strip of the day, Palmer Cox's *Brownies.* Harlow Hoyt in *Town Hall Tonight* describes one such production in Beaver Dam, Wis., in 1896, a ragtag affair directed by a college student.

Around the turn of the century Anna Sara Boch of Minneapolis produced *Union Depot* as well as Tom Thumb weddings with local actors in the Chicago area. The latter used all-children casts in a mock wedding ceremony interspersed with singing and dancing. Tom Thumb weddings were extremely popular into the 1920s.

The first of the large companies, the John B. Rogers Producing Company of Fostoria, Ohio, opened in 1903. John B. Rogers, forced to drop out of the University of Michigan by an injury, was invited by the Knights of Pythias to stage a charity show. After its success he wrote the prototype of many home talent shows thereafter, *Fi-Fi of the Toy Shop.* It was imitative of the familiar *Babes in Toyland.* It had a large cast of adults and children, desirable for optimum audience appeal. Local lodges and clubs could enjoy and take part in it with minimum effort. Fun was the keynote of home talent shows; seldom were there long speeches to memorize or too much strain on any actor.

Soon Rogers had a number of imitators as the home talent idea spread. The quality, however, of many of these shows was uneven. MacKinlay Kantor in memoirs about his boyhood in Webster City, Iowa (around 1914), recalls the "curse" of home talent with its high-pressure salesmanship and often dirty costumes. Kantor played a pig in a costume with a spring-motivated tail and a ring in its snout. Scripts and music were pirated with a few old vaudeville jokes mixed in, he adds.

Jerome H. Cargill, who worked for Rogers around 1920 and today heads Jerome H. Cargill Producing Organization, Inc., of New York City,

summarized some of the other successful operations during the Universal
Producing Company era:

The Joe Bren Company "had about ten men coaches" and
operated out of Chicago. He "did minstrels mostly for Elks and
Shriners." Two Bren directors were Freeman Gosden and Charles
Correll, who would soon attain fame as the radio team *Amos 'n Andy*.

William Dodd Chennery of Springfield, Ill., put on biblical
pageants mostly for churches, using "lots of diamond dye scenery,"
a type that could be rolled up for transport. Two of his shows were
*Ahasuerus* and *Egypta*. An employee, A. Mills Davis, "later took out
his own show," *The College Hero*.

Donald MacDonald of La Crosse, Wis., was "the pioneer
developer of the society market, playing large cities for the Junior
Leagues." Grace Henry and Lila Stuart had companies that followed
his pattern.

Professor Augostini staged an indoor festival in small-town opera
houses which he called "Kermis," the name for annual fairs in the
low countries. His booker Gene Trader took over when the professor
grew too old.

Frederick B. Ingram of Rock Island, Ill., "performed well in
small towns and operated much like the Rogers Company." He had
several dozen young men and women as coaches and produced plays
including *Land of the Honeymoon, Betty Lou, Circus Solly,* and *Sixty
Miles an Hour.*

Moorehead Attractions of Zanesville, Ohio, was headed by sisters
Meda, Edna, and Elizabeth Moorehead, who "got their start after
the First World War. Agnes Moorehead, the actress, was their
niece."

The Sympson Levie Company of Bardstown, Ky., and Jackson,
Mich., staged the popular *Womanless Wedding*. Ruth Hall of
Sergeant Bluff, Iowa, who directed productions for them,
remembers that there were about thirty women directors and three
men who did advance booking. There were, she writes, "no spoken
parts except the Butler and Minister who used cue sheets. . . . The
play was a *novelty* and almost always a sellout."

Bigger than any of these in the 1920s and 1930s was the Wayne P.
Sewell Producing Company of Atlanta, Ga. It staged shows in at least
forty-six states and was especially strong in the Southeast. Wayne P.
Sewell and his wife, Hetty Jane Dunaway Sewell, started in Chautauquas
and, after marriage in 1916, launched their own home talent show com-

pany. Their musical plays included *Here Comes Arabella, Miss Blue Bonnet, Cupid Up-to-Date, The Flapper Grandmother, Oh, Professor!* and *Rosetime.*

Sewell costumes were probably the best in the trade, and their coaches had an idyllic place for their training, a lovely twenty-acre garden that included woodland paths, grottos, pools, an outdoor amphitheater, and a barn theater. Minnie Pearl trained coaches for Sewell in the late 1930s.

Thus as Universal Producing Company started business in the late 1920s it faced strong, widely varied, and ubiquitous competition.

*1,001 Broadways* had two beginnings. The first was made by Franceswayne herself.

Her last home talent show work was with the Empire Producing Company, Kansas City, Mo., headed by George De Haven. "Frannie," writes De Haven, "wrote the shows, arranged the music, supervised our costume department, and designed the costumes, in fact, was the creative entity of the Empire organization. In addition, she trained our directors in the show, dance steps, etc." He believes, "without question" that Franceswayne "contributed more to the content and production values of the home talent show field than anybody."

But by the late 1950s when the fortunes of home talent started downhill, Fran turned her thoughts to writing a book about her experiences, and especially about the formative years of her career with the Universal Producing Company. She enlisted the help of her sister Maxine and her sister's husband, William T. Schoyer, who had been journalists, in editing it. Her boss, George De Haven, also helped with advice and encouragement. Yet her frustrations about getting her flood of memories down on paper are evident from a typewritten fragment among her papers:

"To hell with giving this book a name. Nobody but me, Sis, her long-suffering husband Bill, and George De Haven think I will ever write it." She did record many of the personal adventures that form the core of this book and listed some others but then gave up the project.

The second start on the book was made in Iowa late in 1976. Dr. Lorelei F. Eckey was helping Caroline Schaffner, Curator of the Museum of Repertoire Americana (a museum of the Midwest Old Settlers and Threshers Association, Inc., Mt. Pleasant, Iowa) catalogue play manuscripts. They ran across a copy of one of Universal Producing Company's scripts, *Corporal Eagen,* and Mrs. Schaffner observed that the company suggested an excellent subject for research. She recalled that when she and her late husband Neil had been living hand-to-mouth as touring actors during the Depression, a trade rumor had it that Universal was making a million dollars a year.

Dr. Eckey had a head start on such research because her husband Theodore was from Fairfield. Indeed, he had been in the same high school class as Universal partner Wilson Stewart, and he helped his wife meet a number of Wilson's classmates at their fifty-fifth reunion.

Early research in Fairfield included interviews with the last living Stewart brother, Merle, and the wife of the late Weston Stewart, Helen, as well as with local historians Orville and Mary Prill, who had worked for the Stewarts. Useful information was gleaned from the Fairfield Public Library, especially from past issues of the *Fairfield Ledger*.

Merle Stewart thought that Dr. Eckey ought to find "that playwright" the Stewarts had had, Franceswayne Allen. A letter of inquiry was sent to her hometown newspaper, *The Columbia* (Missouri) *Daily Tribune*. Soon Dr. Eckey received a telephone call from Franceswayne's sister Maxine Allen Schoyer of Pittsburgh, Pa. Mrs. Schoyer said that Franceswayne had died June 4, 1965, but that she had lots of material about her.

Dr. Eckey visited the Schoyers in Pittsburgh in August 1977, and they supplied her with all their Franceswayne memorabilia. This included the memoirs she had written in preparation for her book; her voluminous, detailed letters; incoming correspondence; and much promotional and other data from the Universal days. The three agreed that this material should form the basis for a book on which they would collaborate.

The masses of notes left by Franceswayne required much analysis and follow-up. Sometimes she wrote several versions of an event, fictionalizing some details, since she had been uncertain whether to write her book as nonfiction or fiction. Our first job was to separate actual events from fantasy. In other instances, all we knew of an incident was a descriptive phrase or two linked to the name of a town. Here the task was to piece together the story by going over other memorabilia and trying further means to learn the dates when she visited the town.

A useful source of information was an extensive back file of the *Coaches Bulletin* loaned by the Stewarts. Those for 1928–31 and 1934 contained directives to the coaches; relayed experiences and messages; and listed top coaches, the towns they were playing, and their earnings. The copies of the *Bulletin* revealed the chronological order of some of Fran's show towns and, from time to time, the personal reactions of Fran to her experiences. Such dates made possible the locating of her publicity in newspaper files. This often told much about each show and the circumstances surrounding it.

Visits to Fran's show towns brought additional information. In Plymouth, Ind., nothing came to light in local publications, but the librarian led Dr. Eckey to former Universal coach Theda Fusch (Grant) and former Ingram and Rogers coach Esther Shapiro (Zink). (The latter granted an interview while she was counting money in a department store where she worked, interrupting several times to sing snatches of her show songs.)

Other former Universal coaches wrote Dr. Eckey after she published articles about Universal in the *Des Moines Register* (Jan. 8, 1978) and the *Palimpsest* (Jan./Feb. 1980). One of them, Evelyn Thompson (Gass) of Lake City, Iowa, had been in the same training class as Franceswayne and gave much useful information, including the name of another class-mate from Indianapolis. This led to the location of Martha Pettijohn (Schulze) who recalled why, after Franceswayne had first been rejected as a coach by the Stewarts, they changed their minds.

The *Bulletin,* in a few instances, and lists of 1929 and 1928 classes sent by Billie Cook (Roth) and Wretha Seaton (Gann) supplied other coaches' hometowns. Letters to their local papers sometimes turned up coaches' addresses or information about them. Extensive correspondence led Dr. Eckey to Fran's ex-roommate.

In several instances people were contacted shortly before their deaths, thus preserving memories that would otherwise have been lost. Among these were Merle Stewart; Mary Prill; former coach Sara Mc-Monigle (Kribbs); former Universal booker Ethel Van Hon (Garretson); past president of the Rogers Company, William W. Munsey; and longtime Rogers Company man Harrington Adams, whose notes helped clarify part of Fran's career before Universal.

Dr. Eckey, besides performing the research, drafted the initial manuscript of *1,001 Broadways.* Will Schoyer wrote and edited a substan-tial revision. Maxine Schoyer assisted him and supplied personal memories of her sister.

The authors wish to express special appreciation to all the people who have been helpful. These include many newspaper editors and librarians, especially Jim Rubin of the Fairfield Public Library; Ann Barthlow of the Chadwick Library, Iowa Wesleyan College, Mt. Pleasant; Doris Ann Nor-ris of the Kaubisch Memorial Library, Fostoria, Ohio; Robert A. McCown of the University of Iowa Libraries, Iowa City; Caroline Schaffner of the Museum of Repertoire Americana; and librarians at the Illinois and In-diana state historical archives and the Boston Public Library. Equally helpful were the many who agreed to interviews or sent tapes or letters. And finally there was Theodore Eckey, who listened to many incomplete versions of this book and made sure of their accuracy in observations about Fairfield and the Stewarts.

# 1,001
## BROADWAYS

*Hometown Talent
on Stage*

# ॐ 1 ॐ

# Theatrical Destiny

*Franceswayne Allen* played her first act on Broadway at the age of three. She sat down smack in the middle of Broadway and Ninth Street in Columbia, Mo., and refused to move. "I not doin' home. Do back to Daddy store," she told her black nurse Flora. Autos and farmers' carts, mixed together in that year of 1910, came to a halt. Drivers began to shout or blow horns. Still the formidable tyke would not budge and even stout Flora shrank from physically removing her.

Four blocks away a citizen hustled into the Allen Music Company store. "Wayne," he called to the proprietor, "your daughter's got traffic snarled from Ninth Street to hell and gone. You better come straighten it out."

It took only a few minutes for Wayne Allen to remove the tiny roadblock and set wheels turning again, and while the incident was dismissed as the prank of a spoiled brat, it suggested that Franceswayne's future exploits would draw large audiences and be played out on hometown Broadways across the United States.

All Franceswayne Allen's early life seemed to predestine her for the theater. Her parents lived in the Athens Hotel in Columbia. Here lonely salesmen and other travelers made the bright, appealing youngster the star of the hotel's life, plying her with sodas and candies and heaping gifts around her tree at Christmas time.

She grew up on the fringes of show business. Her father, Wayne Bishop Allen, was proprietor of "the largest music store between St. Louis and Kansas City," where she absorbed blues, jazz, and folk music

3

from her father, musician customers, and black piano movers. If, after arriving home from school, she saw that the family's rosewood Steinway piano was not in place, she knew it had been lent to the University of Missouri for a performance by Schumann-Heink, Paderewski, or another visiting celebrity. She was familiar with her father's composition of local songs such as "Mid the Hills of Old Missouri" and his mastery of musical instruments, since she often attended local entertainments where he performed.

In school she excelled in most subjects and was always active in theatricals, throwing herself into work as well as play with superabundant energy. She took singing, dancing, and elocution lessons and performed in the home talent shows and Tom Thumb weddings staged in town. As a dancing pair, she and her sister so impressed a talent scout that he offered to take them to Hollywood to be in the movies.

Their mother refused. She had been a school principal in College Mound, Mo., and had a good education rather than show business in mind for her daughters. Ione Gibson Allen was a tiny ruler-whacking disciplinarian who could make husky, six-foot farm boys quail. Franceswayne inherited her mother's ability to intimidate others, which was to stand her in good stead later.

She was elected Girl Most Likely to Succeed and president of her senior class at Columbia High School. She attended the University of Missouri where she majored in journalism. She also took dramatic courses at Christian College in Columbia. Her grades were outstanding. She belonged to a social sorority and the women's honor society. She wrote and directed the University's big annual journalism show. She had many friends and a fiancé of distinguished family. The future looked bright.

Then came the day that was to change her life. It fell on a football weekend in the autumn of 1926. Fran had gone to a game in St. Louis with a bevy of friends who were considered the most brilliant, dashing group on campus. There was excitement and spirited mischief in the air. A lively discussion arose. Did shoplifting take any brains? Could anyone get away with it? Some in this gifted group thought so, others did not. A dare was issued for a volunteer. Who but the ringleader, Franceswayne, would accept it? The target was to be nothing that could represent serious theft. How about a pair of stockings? Perfect. Easy to hide, too.

As Fran made her way to the hosiery and glove department of Famous-Barr, she felt carried away by the excitement of the moment and the anticipated adulation of her crowd. To heighten the tension, she pretended to lose her nerve before she palmed her prize.

In this unfamiliar exercise, however, Fran proved less clever than she thought. She was nabbed immediately by a store detective. Soon she was sobbing out the whole story. Her friends vanished like frightened rabbits.

Big city newspapers do not ordinarily report the theft of a pair of stockings; far larger pilferage goes unrecorded daily. Here, however, was a great football weekend human-interest story featuring University of Missouri sorority girls of well-established families in Columbia. A special Sunday edition was run as a sales booster in Columbia, with a banner front-page headline, "M.U. COED TURNS SHOPLIFTER ON DARE."

It is one thing to learn about the power of the press in a University of Missouri journalism course; to be struck down by that power is quite another matter. Fran was devastated and humiliated not only for herself but also for her family. They had to shoulder the burden of her shame almost as if they themselves had taken part in the incident. Franceswayne felt she could not face her teachers, her crowd, or her fiancé. The newspaper story had become her scarlet letter to be worn for life.

Her fiancé, because of his family's influence and his own promising character, appeared headed for a national career. She would not ask him to bear her disgrace which she thought would damage his future. She broke her engagement and fled from Columbia.

That summer she had taken a play-directing course from the John B. Rogers Producing Company of Fostoria, Ohio, which had been in the business of staging home talent shows since 1903. Rogers ran the school to make money during the slack summer season and to provide a pool of directors for the company shows. Now Fran decided to see if Rogers could get her a job.

The job was forthcoming, but it was with an unseasoned organization called Associated Producers. She staged several shows for them before the company went out of business. Then, yielding to her parents' vigorous persuasion, she returned to her home and her college career. She graduated from the University of Missouri in 1928.

She and her fiancé never fitted their broken romance together, although they remained friends and corresponded for years. Resolutely, she put what might have been out of her life. What could fill the void? Franceswayne had grown up wanting to be a star. Further, her smattering of theatrical experience convinced her that no one was more certainly a star than the director of a home talent show.

True, the home talent director did not appear on the stage except as master of ceremonies or to fill an absent actor's role. Regardless, she *was* the show. Without her it could not exist. The sponsoring organization, its show committee, the amateur actors, the contributing businesses, even the stagehands, all depended on her. The show revolved around the coach like the earth around the sun. The coach was "Miss Theater," "Miss

Show Business," the center of a glamorous theatrical universe of make-believe that she created amid otherwise workaday routine in a town. When she rang down the curtain on the world she brought, she frequently departed with gifts and the plaudits of the citizens ringing in her ears.

Fran felt her background eminently fitted her for this glittering world. As she pondered where to begin, she came upon a recruiting advertisement for a new home talent organization, Universal Producing Company of Fairfield, Iowa, run by the Stewart brothers. Soon her application was in the mail.

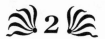

# A Dramatic Course
# Like None Before
# or Since

*Franceswayne Allen* was one of 1,000 young women who worked as dramatic coaches for Universal Producing Company during its decade of operation. But first they had to pass Universal's course in hometown show business, a whip-cracking boot camp of dramatics, unduplicated elsewhere. "This is the nearest thing to joining the army a girl can do," Fran wrote her parents.

Everything about the classes bore the unmistakable imprint of the chief instructor Wilson T. Stewart, a young man in his late twenties. Franceswayne's first letter home from Fairfield, Iowa, described him as "so charged with dynamite, if he jarred himself he'd blow himself to bits. He is the original human dynamo, a composite jumping jack, diplomat, slave driver, matinee idol, top sergeant, rolled into one.

"He can think of a dozen things at once: what tempo he is using to train a dancing chorus, which girl is in or out of step, what his golf score was yesterday, why Goshen, Ind., has not confirmed its contract, which jokes he will spring at the Rotary Club next Thursday, what the seating capacity of the Moose Hall in Saginaw is, where he can get a new foot remedy, and all this while his feet and body are executing the intricate maneuvers of a dance routine." He looked, according to another ex-director, Margarete Gra Morse (Grogan),[1] something like Ramon Novarro.

---

1. Where known, the married name of a coach is given in parentheses when first introduced. Thereafter, her maiden name appears as used on the home talent circuit.

A trainee's first contact with Wilson came in a screening interview before enrollment. It took place typically on a Saturday morning in a midwestern city hotel. The applicant probably clutched an ad from her local paper:

> WANTED COLLEGE GRADUATES to be-
> come Home Talent show directors. Excellent
> opportunity to travel. Can you sing and
> dance? Do you have dramatic ability? Pleas-
> ant work with worthy civic and service or-
> ganizations. Organize, train and produce
> amateur shows. Good salary and commis-
> sion. Traveling expenses guaranteed. Write
> UNIVERSAL PRODUCING CO. Fairfield,
> Iowa.

As she entered the hotel room, she saw a young man of slight but athletic build, with large head, dark complexion, Charlie Chase mustache, and businesslike manner. He asked about the applicant's background, described the company, and made it clear that neither the training nor the work would be easy. To those who passed his inspection he issued the challenge: "If you can do this, you can do anything. I dare you to try." His voice "was masculine, did not soothe or plead, had no style or eloquence, but it commanded," said Margarete Morse. "It told me plainly what I was getting into. Not theater—but show biz."

By winnowing the best from 200 responses to their advertisement, the Stewarts brought together a class of thirty on July 15, 1928, in their first large training course. The students, including Franceswayne, would introduce Universal theatrics to nationwide America.

The first session opened at eight o'clock on a hot morning. The girls gathered in a high-domed old room over a block of stores not far from the square in Fairfield. With military precision Wilson Stewart snapped their last names, "Allen, Fry, Gardner, Pettijohn, Thompson. . . ." He delivered a brief speech about company rules and informed them that a key objective would be to learn to put WHAM into Universal shows. WHAM was what "made the audience laugh, squirm, clap and whis-tle. . . . WHAM lets you eat."

Wilson then launched on the day's routine, vividly brought to life in a voluminous letter Fran wrote her father.

"We begin with work on contracts in case there is some misunder-standing when we arrive in a town. Universal bookers are not out-and-out liars, but their job is to get the contracts signed so we girls will have towns to go into—so maybe they exaggerate a little. We are not to be surprised if the committee expects us to arrive with a minstrel show, a Toby comedian, William Jennings Bryan, or a troupe of elephants and acrobats inside our luggage.''

For the first two hours each morning the class was bombarded by typical committee-member questions. It was up to the students to answer in any manner that would save the contract so the show could go on.

The four Stewart brothers—Raymond, Wilson, Merle, and Weston— took turns at impersonating the types of committee people the directors would meet. They were sweet old ladies who were afraid the proposition was too big for their sewing circle or smart alec American Legion, VFW, or Elks Club big shots who attempted to tell the director what to do. Then the Stewarts pretended to be members of weak organizations with no social standing or city fathers who belonged to the Rotary Club, Kiwanis Club, Chamber of Commerce, or Lions Club and felt they were too busy to help put on a show.

"We learn what to tell them all," Fran wrote. "What to admit, what to skip, and what to laugh off. When to do nothing more than look the person square in the eye and smile. When to take the injured 'I'm just one poor little girl out here alone in the world' attitude. All this in order to sell the proposition. I think these sessions are great good fun. It's like a battle of wits—a gamble—and the best poker face wins."

At ten o'clock the students began learning the play they would produce, *Aunt Lucia*. Every director had to memorize the entire script as well as the voice, walk, posture, and characterization of each role, because on location the amateurs were never allowed to use a script while rehearsing. To teach the lines spoken by an old absent-minded professor, the coach would stoop over, limp, shake her hands, and nod her head as she spoke with a cracked voice. The student would then automatically imitate the characterization as well as the lines. "Sort of a case of monkey see, monkey do, but it is amazing how rapidly lines can be learned by this method," noted Fran.

To teach this technique, the Stewarts sent each student to a different part of the room. For twenty minutes each worked on several pages of a script, saying the lines aloud, gesturing, and walking. Soon all thirty girls were talking at once, some pretending to be black porters, others sophisticated society matrons, others college cheerleaders or butter-and-egg men (rural bigshots). "To see them all jabbering, hopping, yelling, slinking, or strutting as the character demands, must give one the impression he has walked into a lunatic asylum," Fran wrote.

Next the students were divided into groups in which each took turns doing all parts. Later each student took a turn at directing others. "Wils

[Stewart] roamed the room, observing and helpfully correcting mistakes. But woe betide the girl who became mixed up; on her his wrath quickly descended. This went on until 12 o'clock."

After lunch came a several-hour session on how to persuade people to take part in the show. Wilson pretended he was a prominent business-man, and the students asked him to dress in skirts, rolled hose with rib-bon garters, wig, or picture hat to impersonate Clara Bow, Peaches Browning, or Tillie the Toiler. Sometimes he was very polite and cool, but firm. Again he was grouchy, or timid and embarrassed. Or he would say, "Sure, Blondie, I'll be in the show if you'll have a date with me tonight. How about it?"

"Then you have to get *out* of the date but still get the man *into* the show without letting him realize what has happened," Fran explained.

She enjoyed the process. "I get a big kick out of this interviewing, because I am actually pretending Wils is some of the dignitaries back home on Broadway like Sam Hunt the banker or Tom Heath the druggist. Yet, after this training class, I feel I could talk any of them, including a couple of local preachers and maybe an MU dean or two, into doing this nonsense."

But not everyone could cope with the interviews. Students who said the wrong thing or simply stood there stumped provoked a Wilsonian ex-plosion. "So you think you're going to be a director, do you?" Wils screamed. "You are going to let some small-town businessman tell you he isn't interested in your show. You're licked, sister! You're standing there with a face a mile long. No wonder he wouldn't listen. Nobody would. You may think you are a director, but I think you're lousy."

If the girl started to cry, she got both barrels from Wils: "Oh, so you are going to blubber about it? Someone has hurt your itsy-bitsy feelings. Now isn't that just too bad. Is that what you are going to do when you get out in a town on your own and things get a little tough: bawl like a crybaby, huh? Well, if you do, you might just as well pack your clothes and go home right now! You won't have anybody's shoulder out there to cry on—nobody is going to wipe away your tears. So stop that damn sniff-ing and go out to the restroom and bathe your face and come back in here with a smile on it."

"Dad, he's never talked that way to me yet, and, by Golly, he just bet-ter not try it," commented Fran. "After all, I'm an Allen, and if he did my Irish temper wouldn't stop, as you well know."

The last two hours of the afternoon were spent in learning how to in-terview the newspaper editor or reporter and what prices should be paid the job printer for window cards, tickets, handbills, and programs. This continued until six o'clock, when the class had an hour for supper. The trainees wolfed their food and ran home to clean up for the night session of singing and dancing. This began at seven o'clock and usually continued until about ten-thirty.

Fran wrote: "Some of the girls are real sharp on the business end of the deal, but they have never danced a step in their lives. Such a sight this chorus line of all shapes and sizes presents as it tries to keep on the same foot as Wilson calls the count! Thanks to you and Mother and Miss Emily Price's dancing school, I have no trouble on dance routines. As to the choruses, you know I can't carry a tune in a basket, but I can shout good and loud, and this seems to be the general idea. 'Don't sing good . . . sing loud . . . shout . . . yell . . . get your voices out' is what the Stewarts scream over and over."

Then came an especially rough night. Wilson, angry at the listless way one student was leading another in a dance, leaped into center floor, shoved the slow student away and grabbed her partner. He dragged her back and forth over the room in a hilarious, bounding dance that left the poor girl in a state of complete exhaustion.

It was beastly hot, and one girl fainted. But Wilson would not be turned aside from his teaching any more than that admiral who said "Damn the torpedos, full speed ahead!" Fran reported. As the whole class, drenched with sweat, gathered around the prostrate form, Wilson yelled, "What is this? Does it take twenty-nine people to revive one? The rest of you get in this chorus line and leave her alone. She's just passed out, that's all. She'll be all right in a minute. Forget her and get your line straight and take that opening number again."

When a second girl passed out he shouted, "Good Lord, what am I supposed to be running, a hospital or a training school?"

Nobody dared move, much less answer.

Then he shouted, "Don't stand there like a bunch of wooden soldiers. Sit down. Shut your mouths. Relax. Don't say a word for ten minutes, and the girl closest to the one on the floor, get her on her feet and give her an aspirin."

Ten minutes later to the second, he was calling, "All right, break it up. Come on out here and let's see you put something into this chorus number. Hey, Marguerite, you there at the piano, give me the introduction slow and retard those first three notes of the chorus . . . ready and . . . one, two. . . ."

Within thirty seconds, thirty students, including the two who had swooned, were swaying in rhythm. They called each step of the chorus in unison, "right hop—left hop—right hop—right, left, right, hop; left hop—right hop—left, right, left, hop." "This is the basis of the old soft shoe," Fran interjected in her letter.

The class danced for about three minutes and then someone missed a hop or a right or a left, and Wilson, who was dancing in front of the line with his back toward the students so they could watch and imitate, bellowed without turning around, "No, no, no, no, no. You, there, third from the end, you're out of step. Stop, stop. Everybody cut."

The accompanist Marguerite Wells, the one person on the whole training staff with whom Franceswayne never developed empathy, left the melody in mid-air, threw up both hands with a pained expression, and drawled, "Oh, now really!"

Wils whirled around to face the offending dancer. "Did you ever go to school?" he demanded.

Thunderstruck, the girl, nodded in the affirmative.

"Well, where were you the day they taught you the difference between your right and left foot? Out to lunch probably." He looked her up and down scornfully and with an exasperated sigh wheeled around again in front of the line. "Okay, we are going to take it again and again and again, till every mother's daughter of you can do it standing on her head. Now, straighten your line—throw your shoulders back—suck in your stomachs, and let's see you smile. Okay, retard the first three notes . . . ready and . . . one, two. . . ."

Here Fran broke off her report because she had to dash to a session where they would be taught how to do the financial checkup and make company reports. This was "interesting in a dull sort of way but I'm sure quite necessary too." She concluded with an Allenesque summary of the curriculum: "So for now, this is all from your daughter who has, within two weeks, turned into a teacher, preacher, salesman, dramatic coach, nursemaid and governess, newspaper reporter, dance-hall queen, sideshow barker and banker."

# 3

# One Little, Two Little, Three Little Indians

*After the first* five days of Universal's training course, six of the students couldn't take it and quit. A steady attrition had begun.

One morning the temperature registered 104°F. "Honestly, it was hotter than the blowtorch used to weld the hinges of hell," wrote Franceswayne. The Stewarts had instructed the class to spend half an hour reviewing the previous day's lectures. However, with no teacher in sight, all the would-be directors slumped into a stupor. Some girls at the second-floor windows gasped for air, pushing wet, straggling hair behind their ears and mopping sweaty faces. Others sprawled on their stomachs on the davenports, hose rolled down to their ankles and skirts pulled up to ventilate their fannies. Others lolled in chairs.

Suddenly the door banged open. There stood a rigid and glaring Wilson Stewart without coat, tie, or shave.

Instantly yawning lips closed, hose came up, skirts came down, and notebooks flew open. Squeaking and scraping chairs mingled with coughs and throat clearings.

Wilson strode to the center of the broken half-circle, looking at no one but seeing them all. Then he exploded. "All right, I have something to tell you pampered and petted mamma's girls. If you don't like what I'm saying, then get the hell out of here! It doesn't matter a damn to me whether any of you ever work for us or not. In fact, I'd rather send the whole bunch of you back home and write letters to your families stating you are lazy, incompetent, and boy crazy than let you go out on the road representing my company and acting like a bunch of cheap two-bit . . . well, I won't say it, but men have a word for women like that, and you're all old enough to know what I'm thinking!"

"Honestly, Dad, you can't imagine the silence in the room after he made that last remark," wrote Fran. "Sitting in that semicircle you could feel the heat wave of blushes generated by those twenty-four girls. All eyes were riveted on notebooks, nervous hands, or cracks in the floor."

Then his manner changed. In a conversational, confidential tone, he continued, "In other words, girls, I'm getting around to this. It has been reported to me by some of the landladies that several of you have been going out on dates with the town boys around here. Furthermore, you have been staying out until five o'clock in the morning. Now if you think you can work in this training class fourteen hours a day and then go chasing around all over hell's half-acre the rest of the night, you are wrong. In the first place, it is physically impossible to do it. In the second place, by God, I won't have it. So if you feel you have to have a lot of loving, petting, and necking in order to live, then the thing for you to do is to go home or some place where you can get it. It's a damn cinch you won't get it from me or anyone else around here that amounts to anything."

Someone in the class chortled. Wilson wheeled with the suddenness of an uncoiled spring. Eyes blazing, nostrils quivering, and jaw set so firmly that the cords of his neck protruded as if they would break through the swarthy column of his throat, he snarled through distorted lips.

"Laugh. That's right, go ahead and laugh! It's damn funny, isn't it! Yeah, I'm funny, the company's funny! What the hell, the whole world's funny. So why don't you laugh?"

Then he threw back his head and roared. His laugh wasn't musical or hearty. It was a horrible sound, "like an ogre in one of my childhood nightmares," Fran wrote. "Dad, it was terrible—yet it was magnificent!"

The laugh ceased as abruptly as it had begun. His voice became low-pitched as he told how the company was a dream he and his brothers, Raymond the general manager, Merle, and Weston, had built from nothing. They had had no financial backing. They had worked hard. They had come a long way and had plans that would mean big things to everyone associated with them in the future. They had faith in their students or they would not have chosen them from hundreds of applicants.

"But let me tell you something right now, and I don't want a girl in this room to ever forget it. Any man with an average brain, a shoeshine, and a bunch of smutty stories can be a traveling salesman. But it takes a damn clever, smart, alert, and intelligent woman to make a success of a traveling job."

Then he paused for his second wind and gave a wry, sly smile, "which we know," commented Franceswayne, "means he is ready to take us by the hand and lead us into still waters."

Now grinning, he said, "I guess by now most of you know our dad was a preacher, and sometimes I get wound up just to prove to myself I'm still my father's son. But seriously, you who carry the title of director will always be—in the minds of men, women and children alike—part of the magical inner circle of the theater. To them you are a 'show girl.' So it naturally follows that these small sheiks want to reap their share of glory by taking you out, so they can come back and brag and joke about what happened, true or not. So if you go out with a fellow like that, you have identified yourself as a person who doesn't particularly care what the best people in town think of you. Understand, not all you girls are included in this mess. But it doesn't hurt you to know the kind of situation that awaits you both here and on the road. Further, since some of you have acted like kids, I'm going to treat you that way. Mark my words, the next girl in class who is seen talking to any man, other than my brothers or me, will be fired from training. Forty-five minutes for lunch. Class dismissed."

After lunch five more girls were missing. "So it looks like the shoe fit some of the sisters," wrote Fran. Class enrollment had now dropped to nineteen. It's getting to be like the song "One little, two little, three little Indians," Fran wrote.

Meanwhile, she had found two friends who helped make the course more enjoyable. One was her roommate, Ethel Jeanne Gardner (Powell), who had a good figure, lots of clothes, and a fine sense of humor. She always seemed to be winking at the world over some private joke. She wore her hair in a swirl down the left side and had a smile as wide as a golden wheatfield in her own Sunflower State. The other, Isabel Jane Fry (Booth), was "witty, friendly as a St. Bernard, and subtle as Machiavelli," as Fran described her. Isabel Jane had formerly worked for a rival producing company, so she knew the fundamentals of the business. When the Stewarts started to sound off on some big theory, she would sometimes stop them cold with a sharp, practical question. These three were less fearful of the Stewarts than the other girls seemed to be.

One day the threesome returned early from lunch and noticed a luxury car outside the entrance. Curious, they tiptoed up the narrow staircase that led to the training rooms and slipped in to watch.

Wilson, his back to the door, was in conversation with a woman or, rather, she was complaining loudly to him. Meanwhile, her Pomeranian dog kept nipping at Wilson's feet; her chauffeur stood by passively; and one of the girls from the class, undoubtedly her daughter, cowered nearby.

The girl was rather ineffectual, a "wash-out" in the vernacular of the time, with a whiny voice. She had from the first pretended to be more sophisticated than she was, thus subjecting herself to barbed comments from the Stewarts. That culminated on a day when she had been criticized for her work, her appearance, her attitude, and her lack of ability. Humiliated, she had made a long-distance call to her mother, who had come to Fairfield to get her little girl and was planning to sue Universal.

Wilson stood quite still while the mother bombarded him with abuse. She accused him of being uncouth, uncivilized, and unprincipled, subjecting her flesh and blood to ungentlemanly conduct for personal gain. She knew her rights, for after all she was "of the theater" herself. She had once been offered the role of Little Buttercup in a Gilbert and Sullivan operetta.

The three eavesdroppers bit their tongues to keep from laughing. The woman was ample of figure, with overpainted face, plucked eyebrows, and perspiring arms heavy with bracelets. Fran's imagination pictured her more naturally in a beef-trust burlesque chorus than in an operetta. Through it all, Wilson remained ominously silent, but the three noticed that the cords in his neck were engorged.

The woman continued. She told how her family had forced her to marry instead of following the way of the footlights. But now her great talent for the stage had been inherited by her beloved daughter. "For this reason, and no other, I allowed my daughter to attend this Universal Producing Company dramatic school."

"Oh," said Wilson. He smiled ingratiatingly. "I'm so glad to know all of this, for I see we have both made a great mistake. You are right. Your daughter undoubtedly does have great undiscovered dramatic talent. But, through some unaccountable mistake, she came up here thinking that we were giving dramatic training for the stage. This is not true. We do teach dramatics, but only as a sideline to prospective teachers or directors who one day may work with amateurs. They are not those seeking to star upon the professional stage."

The mother grew calmer. "Really?" she picked up the dog.

"Now, since you have been so kind as to explain your background and the aspirations of your daughter, I can see where she might have been led to believe that our methods were a little harsh. Undoubtedly one with a fine and sensitive soul such as she possesses belongs to art—yes, to the theater in its highest form." He started to usher them down the stairway. "I am so indebted to you for your visit," he said. "And, under the circumstances, I suggest that you take your daughter home with you now. There is no time to be lost if you would launch her career on Broadway for this season."

The woman beamed from her crepe-lidded eyes, patted Wilson's arm with her stubby, coral-enameled claws, and cooed, "Ah, Mr. Stewart, they don't do you justice when they describe you. You are really quite charming and understanding, and so perceptive to recognize my dear daughter's talent."

As Wilson waved farewell to the departing limousine, the three friends doubled over with belly laughs. Yet almost immediately, Wilson tore up the stairs, two at a stride, and the girls attempted to stifle their giggles with their handkerchiefs. His eyes were twinkling. He was biting the skin around his right thumb, a sign that he was either making a great decision or concealing merriment. But as he saw the girls, his manner changed.

"What?" he barked, looking at them ferociously. "Didn't I give you an hour for lunch? What the hell are you doing back so early? Did you come to spy on me? Well, if so, you know by now how I feel about Little Buttercups who are cheating Broadway. For the record, just let me tell you three smart jacks that there is a train leaving for New York in forty-five minutes. So in case there are any vacant seats when I call the roll, I'll know where to forward your mail."

Then he grinned with a look like a little boy with his hand caught in the jam jar and said, "On the other hand, kids, it's hotter than hades up here, and you still have five minutes for some fresh air while I grab a cup of coffee." With that he turned and bounded down the steps, three at a time.

Following "Little Buttercup's" departure, and as the burning midsummer heat continued, three more "little Indians" dropped out. This left a class of fifteen, exactly half the original enrollment.

Three nights before the end of the course, the class learned makeup. Wilson, his brothers, and Marguerite put juvenile makeup on each other, which the girls had to copy by applying it to a classmate. Then the students did character makeups with mustaches, whiskers, and sideburns.

After four or five gluings and ungluings of such appendages had swelled and reddened tender skins, Fran led the howls of protests at the announcement they were to do black face. But W.T. stood firm. Soon there was a roomful of wide, white, greasepaint mouths, like sugar doughnuts on the raw faces. Then came the cool, moist burnt cork. As it was applied, groans turned into giggles.

After inspection, Raymond ended the class. "Okay, you dirty-faced dolls, that'll be all for tonight. It's only 2:00 A.M. Usually this takes us until about 4:00. So you've got six hours. Be back here at 8:00 with your faces clean. Class dismissed!"

Two-thirds of the girls, too tired to remove this last makeup, decided to eat at Mel's Cafe. Never before had so many of them gone there together, but tonight seemed different. Tonight blondes, brunettes, redheads, and two girls with silver in their tresses huddled together, their burnt-cork faces marked here and there by grooves of white where tears had trickled, calling for pork tenderloins, hamburgers with onions, and coffee—coffee black, coffee with cream, *coffee*! Then Isabel Jane, with the best singing voice in the group, started the show's opening song. That did it. From then on, they all whooped and hollered their way through every number in *Aunt Lucia,* on key or off, with Fran's deep voice under-pinning them all.

What a wonderful feeling! No Stewart—and especially no W.T.—was in sight. A spirit was beginning to form among them, a feeling of kinship.

It was three in the morning when they left Mel's. But they felt ex-hilarated. Perhaps one or two of them thought of Wilson's challenge in that first interview, "I dare you to try," and answered, "Well, you can see I did!"

# ◈ 4 ◈

# Judgment Day

*Franceswayne didn't go* right to bed when she returned to her boarding house. She was too excited. Instead she wrote a long letter to her father. Consequently she had only about an hour's sleep before class. All, including the Stewarts, were half-asleep, grouchy, edgy, and uncooperative. Wilson started the class by announcing that there was nothing new to learn. Most of them had already memorized the script. Now they would have a review.

As the class droned on and Wilson asked question after question about things they had learned almost three weeks before, Fran, Isabel, and Ethel Jeanne began a private game of tick-tack-toe. For a while they hid the fact by passing the paper back and forth in time with their affirmative or negative nods to his obvious questions. They weren't really paying attention, and, as Fran discovered that she was about to win three in a row, she became careless and nodded a wrong answer.

Suddenly she realized that the room was deathly quiet. She looked up inquiringly, never suspecting that she was the cause. She had never been the focus for any of the Stewarts' barbs.

Wilson told her to stand. Later, she didn't remember doing so, but she did remember looking in bewilderment at the faces turned toward her. For a minute nothing happened, but as she stood there she felt like Lady Godiva with a boyish bob and no horse in sight.

Then Wilson focused his eyes on her, flailed his arms, and screamed in full voice, "All right, Allen, you think you're pretty wise-headed, don't you? You graduated from university this year, so you have the world by the tail on a downhill pull. Ha! You think your diploma will automatically make you a success wherever you go. Ha! And you think your family is really something, too, don't you?"

At the mention of her family, Fran felt the blood rising in her face.

"Well, you're all wrong, little girl. A degree is something to plead guilty to, not brag about. The same goes for your precious family connections. And the sooner you get the idea out of your head that you're pretty clever and pretty superior, the better off you'll be. You're not clever. You're just a dumb little nitwit who has been babied and pampered all your life by your precious mamma and daddy."

Fran's Irish temper erupted. "That's not so!" she yelled.

"That's not so," he mimicked. "Yeah, if it wasn't so, you'd be able to use your head and think for yourself when asked a question. But no. You depend on your sorority and your family to get you by. Ha! When you come against a proposition in the real world, where you're required to stand on your own, you'll just melt like a sugar cube. You haven't the guts, little girl, you haven't the guts."

Fran was boiling. Her eyes blazed. But her voice was low, cool, and deliberate. Before she knew it, she was walking—stalking—slowly toward him, talking as she went.

"Well," she said, punctuating each word with a step, "I've got guts enough to tell you, Wils Stewart, that your yelling doesn't scare me. And I know how to yell as loud as you. And even though I was brought up not to swear. . . ." She put her hands on her hips and held her chin high as she stood scarcely three feet away. "Damn it! If that's what it takes to get this job done, I can do that, too."

He started to say something, but Fran shook her head violently and blasted, "Don't interrupt me. I'm not through with you yet. I came here to learn this business because I wanted to. I paid good money because I wanted to. If I knew all there was to know about it, there'd be no reason for my being here. And one more thing." Her whole body was tense. "Don't you ever, and I mean *ever,* say anything against my family again. I WON'T HAVE IT!"

At that, she slapped him solidly across the face. The thunderclap sounded in her ear, and her fingers stung as she started back toward her seat. She heard him behind her. She expected him to knock her flat on her face, but she didn't care. Instead, he caught up with her and, almost gently, took her by the arm.

"Wait a minute, there, gal. I had you figured all wrong." Then, with an irresistible boyish smile, he offered his hand and said, "Here, shake."

He turned to the rest of the class, who were gaping at the scene. "You know, this gal has spunk. In fact, she's got more stuff than I thought. Instead of backing down or crying like a lot of you would have done, she has the backbone to stand up for her rights. That's what it takes when you're on the road. If you give the other fellow a chance, he'll run over you every time.''

He dismissed the class for three hours, bounded out the door, and disappeared down the steep steps. Fran sank into a chair and shook. Girls patted her on the back and congratulated her. That was exactly what this Wils needed, wasn't it? It should have been done long ago.

The only one who didn't agree was Marguerite the piano player. She and Fran, had been at odds from the first. "Look," she said, facing the group, "I don't understand your attitude at all. I don't think that what Miss Allen did was commendable. It was a disgraceful display of bad manners. You may think Mr. Stewart has overlooked it. But if you knew him as well as I do, you would know that he will never forgive or forget such an insult. So beware, girls. Beware!'' Marguerite left.

For a moment Fran thought of the smooth way that Wilson had disguised his feelings when he talked to the society matron who had once been asked to play Little Buttercup. But this was different, wasn't it? She dismissed the uneasiness she felt, or tried to. She decided to do the best she could for the last two days of class.

Those days passed without incident.

Then came judgment day in August 1928. This was when the Stewarts were to announce to each trainee, in an individual interview, her appointment or rejection as coach. The night before, the Stewarts and Marguerite had been up late, pacing back and forth, discussing the qualifications of the fourteen girls now left in the class. Their task was to decide who would get the dozen towns for which they had bookings.

The first girl entered the room at eight the next morning. What happened followed a pattern repeated with each student. Raymond, behind the desk, looked at her carefully. Point by point, he talked about her three weeks of classwork. In painstaking detail, he told her what was wrong with her speaking, her singing, and her technique for handling amateur actors. Maybe she was too easily ruffled. Maybe her manner was too apologetic or too proud. After recounting faults, Raymond handed her the name of a town and started listing her strong points. Finally he welcomed her into the organization by saying that if she did as well on the road as she did in class, she'd build a good career.

Each girl left that room with the mingled emotions of a life-termer who has been paroled and a big game hunter who was setting out to stalk a white leopard. Some girls felt that they should have been given bigger towns, whereas others were scared to death because they got big ones.

All Fran's friends were looking up bus and train schedules with shining eyes, wiring their parents for pocket money, and making appointments for shampoos, manicures, and marcels. They gathered briefly in Gaumer's Drugstore before going back to their boarding houses to pack. There they told the girls who were still waiting anxiously about their assignments.

Isabel Jane Fry got Rock Island, Ill. Ethel Jeanne Gardner got Harrisonville, Mo., near Kansas City. Evelyn Thompson (Gass) was on her way to Morganfield, Ky., and Lois Lawler to Coleman, Ala. They would go as far as Nashville together and share a watermelon. And Martha Pettijohn (Schulze), a doctor's daughter from Indianapolis, Ind., departed for Washburn, Ill.

By noon, Fran had seen many of the girls off with promises to write or call and a tearful exchange of presents.

As the hours passed, Fran's excitement mounted. She spent most of the day at the drugstore to get the latest news from each girl. She became more and more curious about what her town would be. East or west, north or south, large or small, she didn't care, as long as she could work. Then she'd show everyone what Franceswayne Allen of Columbia, Mo., could do!

She was to have the last interview of the day at four. In her mind, they had saved the best for last. It took forever for four to arrive. Finally she could wait no longer. At ten minutes before the hour, heart pounding with anticipation, she left the wild hysteria and the final, shouted goodbyes, raced to the office, and climbed the steps deliberately as though she were about to make a grand entrance on stage.

But Raymond wasn't there. Nor was Wilson nor Merle nor Pete. Instead, sitting at the desk was Marguerite. Fran's heart sank. Why was Marguerite the only one on this day of days, this hour of hours?

"Oh, you're the eager one, aren't you?" the woman smirked as Fran walked in. "Well, no matter. It's just as well." She paced her words so that each one would have its full effect. "You see, you are the last of the girls, and we asked you to come in a little late for a particular reason."

"Why, that's all right," Fran said as politely as she could. "I didn't mind waiting a bit. Except I'm nearly popping with curiousity to know what town my first show will be in."

Marguerite hunched her shoulders. Then, even more slowly and deliberately and with a fake southern accent, she said, "But, my deah, that's the point. We aren't giving you a town. We aren't sending you out on a show."

Fran choked. "Oh, Miss Wells." Surely the woman was teasing her, trying to get in one last dig before one of the Stewarts came with the truth. After all, it wasn't four o'clock yet.

Then she found herself saying, "I've just got to have a town. I've just got to."

"Now, my deah," drawled Marguerite, "let's not get emotional, overwrought, or hysterical about this. I am probably doing you the greatest favor of your life. Right now you may not see it that way, but someday you will thank me."

Fran looked over to the door hoping . . . hoping . . . hoping . . . hoping that a Stewart would walk in and set things straight. But no one came. Tears welled in her eyes and started down her cheeks. She sobbed and snuffled, not able to even look at her antagonist. All she saw was a big, black ink spot on the green blotter in front of her.

When she finally found her voice, a torrent of words gushed out. She kept repeating, "You don't know what this means to me. You couldn't know. Nobody really knows. More than anything in the world, I want to be a director. And I *can* be a good one, I know. The best there is."

"Now, my deah, you are young, and you have your whole life ahead of you. And it can be a good life. You must believe me when I tell you that we have considered your case very thoroughly. All of us decided you are simply not good director material."

"What did I do that made you decide this?"

"It isn't so much what you did do as what you haven't done. You see, to be a director—one worthy of Universal Producing Company—a girl must have many sides to her personality. She will be asked to meet many challenges once she is out on her own. She must be stable and dependable, no matter what the emergency. Let us say, perhaps, that your youth is one of the factors involved. Someday when you are a little more mature, perhaps you can come back and go through the school again and then maybe. . . ."

She went on and on and on. The gist was that Fran was too stupid and unstable to be trusted to put on a show for the company. Fran stood it for as long as she could. If this piano-thumping, conniving Marguerite thought that she was going to go home and take up dressmaking or nursing, she was mistaken.

"It's just not fair. What you're saying isn't true. I know more about what I can do than you do," she burst out. "I demand to see the Stewarts. Where are they?"

"The boys have gone. They left the office about half an hour ago."

Marguerite suggested that Fran go back to her room, pack, and take the midnight train back to Columbia to that nice father and mother she was so fond of. She concluded by saying "I want you to know that this hasn't been easy for me. So please don't think too harshly of me. But I've done and said what I have for your own good." She stood and switched off the light.

Fran turned and started from the office, moaning softly, "But you don't understand. You will never understand. I can't go home. I just can't."

She opened the outer door. Wanting no one to see her, she used the back streets to make her way to her boarding house, biting her lips to keep from crying and silently chanting, "Damn Marguerite Wells. I hate her. I hate her. I have always hated her."

When she got to her room, she locked the door and fell across the bed, sobbing and pounding her fists in the pillow. It was true that one other girl hadn't been given a town, but no one had really expected her to make it. She was the dumbest girl in the class. It was bad not to be chosen, but to be put in the same category with that other girl—well, there was something wrong somewhere. It was simply not fair!

Then Fran thought of the other girls who had made it. There were at least three older ones whom she was sure didn't know beans-with-the-bag-open about directing. They merely wanted a chance to catch a man. They had even told the other girls that. No one in the training class was as serious about making a career as Franceswayne Allen was. So why had she not been chosen?

Finally when she felt cried out, she decided to call her father. Maybe if she could talk to him, everything would be all right. Goodness knows, she needed some kind of sympathy. She wiped her face and picked up the phone. Mabel the maid answered. Fran heard her tell the operator, "Yessum, this is the Wayne B. Allen residence. I am Mabel the cook. I am the onliest one that is here. Mr. and Miz Allen, they both took off and went to Brushwood Lake to the cabin afishin' and they won't be home before Sunday midnight."

Fran had never felt so empty and alone. She thought of getting something to eat, but she wasn't hungry. But she could at least write a letter. Then they'd know what had happened to her when she either disappeared or killed herself. She simply couldn't go back home and face all the girls in the crowd and everybody in town who had believed in her. That was the one thing she could not do.

Meanwhile in Washburn, Ill., Martha Pettijohn had wrestled her trunk off the tracks and walked into town to find lodging with a dear old lady and, although it was late in the afternoon, had launched her first coaching assignment. She began at the barber shop where the owner consented to be her leading man. Proceeding down the street to assemble more of her cast, she suddenly—maybe dragging that trunk had something to do with it—was stricken with appendicitis.

The phone rang at the Stewart house. Raymond answered. "What?" he said. "Pettijohn can't do the show? She's gone home? Well, we'll send another coach to Washburn right away." He hung up.

Now where in the hell was he going to get another coach? All the girls had been sent out, he and his brothers were tied up, and the next class of coaches hadn't even arrived for training. Then he thought of Franceswayne. The train for Columbia didn't leave until midnight. Perhaps she was still in town.

Fran could hardly believe what she heard when he phoned her. "Allen? Gee, Allen, I'm sure glad you haven't left town. I don't know what in the world I would do if I hadn't gotten in touch with you." Raymond sounded relieved, pleasant, and friendly. He asked her to meet him at his office immediately.

Fran dashed cold water on her swollen face. Even though her eyes looked red from crying, by the time she had patted on some powder and used the new lipstick that Ethel Jeanne had given her, she was almost the old Fran.

She ran through the twilight, taking a shortcut through the park in the center of the square. She stumbled and fell, skinning her knee and tearing her last pair of silk Gold Stripe hosiery. "What the hell?" she thought. She took the steps to the office eagerly, and when she opened the door, there was big Raymond smiling broadly.

The first thing he said was, "Allen, how would you like to stage a show in Washburn, Illinois?"

"Honest?" She practically shouted with joy. "Do you mean it? Can I really?"

"Sure. I think you can, or I wouldn't send you out there."

"But I thought," she stammered, "that is, Miss Wells said. . . ."

"I know all about that," he interrupted jovially. "Forget everything she said. We've got to get down to business and get you out of town and on your way in less than two hours to get you there before morning. This Washburn is a tough town, but it can be a good one if you give it enough time and start early tomorrow. You are the one girl I know who can do it."

Fran felt a real sense of gratitude for Raymond Stewart. The others might not have appreciated her, but he was *the* general manager. He could step in and correct their mistakes.

"Oh, yes, one more thing," he said. "Be sure you make at least $100 for the company. If you do, we'll give you another town."

"You bet," she promised. There was no doubt in her mind that she could make at least that much if not much, much more. All she needed was a chance.

"Whoopee," the newly accredited coach repeated over and over to herself as she ran back across the square to pack.

# ≋5≋

# Off on the Home
# Talent Adventure

*Raymond delivered* her costume trunk to the station and Fran caught the night train for Peoria and changed there to a spur line.

Fellow passengers on the coach rocking through the midwestern darkness would have seen her as physically well endowed, with reddish brown hair. Snapping, large brown eyes and small, rosebud mouth accented a thin face. To Fran's mind the conductor had been eyeing her as if he thought she was too young to be traveling alone late at night. Now he pulled out his watch.

"You aren't planning to get off at Washburn, are you?" he asked.

Fran's bright eyes flickered with surprise. Of course she was. No matter that she was alone, that she had never been to Washburn, that she had been unable to arrange a place to stay, and that she would be alighting at two-thirty in the morning.

The conductor peered over his spectacles at her in a fatherly way. "Someone going to meet you?"

"No."

"You know anyone there?"

She choked down a rising annoyance. "Not yet," she admitted, standing up to take full advantage of her five-foot-six-inch height. "But it won't be long before I know everyone in town. I'm going there on business. I represent the Universal Producing Company." She started to reach for her bag, but his restraining hand fell on her arm.

"I can't let you off there, young lady. Not alone in the middle of the night," he said.

"I must get off. The Women's Club is counting on me to be there in the morning to put on a big show for them!"

The conductor shook his head. He warned her that this town was tough.

"That doesn't worry me," Fran retorted.

He told her of the convict camp located only one block from the depot.

"That has nothing to do with me," she answered. "I don't care a diddley-squat about your convicts!"

Her eyes began to smoulder, a sign of the lashing temper that would become the terror of many a would-be actor who blew lines. Before sparks could fly, the conductor stated flatly that it would be too dangerous for her to detrain, and walked off down the aisle.

After a moment of thought, Fran began to examine the windows. Could she get one open, thrust her bag through, and jump if the train slowed in Washburn? No. There was still the costume trunk. Not much packed in it this trip—only an oversized gray wig, a two-piece black dress, and a dozen little sailor outfits. But losing these or the new trunk would spell the end of her career with Universal.

All right. It was up to her to change the conductor's mind. But the threatened scene evaporated when the conductor returned smiling.

"It's okay," he said. "I've fixed things for you, young lady. In the smoker I found another passenger who's getting off at Washburn. He'll be your chaperone."

Descending to the platform at two-thirty, Fran watched as the freight hands tossed down her trunk. The train chugged off, and she and her chaperone were alone. In the fitful illumination of heat lightning, Franceswayne's companion appeared so small that she wondered if he were not a young boy.

Nevertheless, when she expressed concern about leaving the trunk lying there in full view, he helped her tumble it along the platform into concealment in a clump of bushes by the road. There was no hotel in sight. She had no choice but to go straight to the home of the president of the Women's Club, sponsors of her first Universal show. Her escort volunteered to lead her to the house, which he said was at the edge of town. He picked up her bag and she followed.

As they walked, she became increasingly puzzled about her companion. He was at least two heads shorter than she. He was, in fact, a dried-up wart of a chap. His movements were jerky, but, with unexpected courtesy, at each corner he lit matches so she would not step into the puddles left by recent rains. In the flare of the match she noticed that his nose was warped into an unusual shape and his eyes twitched rapidly. Could he be one of the convicts the conductor had warned her about? All the while he kept up cheerful, reassuring chatter. He said he had lived in Washburn since childhood and that it was a nice town. He was glad to be home again.

Finally they reached a big rambling farmhouse set deep on a lawn surrounded by towering oaks. A dog began barking, and as they drew closer, a shutter creaked. Suddenly the dog charged and, growling ferociously, seized the leg of Fran's escort. The little man let out a howl that fairly drowned the dog's racket, shook his leg loose, threw her suitcase into the yard, and fled, pursued by the dog. (Franceswayne never saw him again, but the next morning she learned that he was an inmate who had escaped, not from the prison, but from an insane asylum.)

A light appeared in the house. Moments later on an upper balcony, Fran could make out a woman in a long white nightgown, her hair done up in kid curlers. She carried a lantern in one hand and a shotgun in the other.

"Is this the home of the president of the Women's Club?" shouted Franceswayne.

"Go away or I'll shoot," the woman quavered.

Fran retreated behind an oak. "I'm Franceswayne Allen," she called from her position of relative safety. "I'm the coach from the Universal Producing Company. I've come to put on the show for you."

There was a long pause. "Judge isn't home," the woman's voice finally said, "and I don't unlock the door until daylight. Can't afford to take any chances with these convicts around here."

"But I can't stay under this tree all night. I'll be chewed up by chiggers!"

Again there was silence. Then, "No, I suppose you can't. I'll tell you what. You just go up on the porch and make yourself comfortable in the hammock until daylight." At that, out went the light and all was quiet again.

Such a welcome to home talent might have dampened some spirits, but not Fran's. She managed a few hours sleep on the porch. The judge's wife proved to be less of an ogre in the morning. And, in a manner typical of her, Fran set about producing her first Universal show as though she had been professionally directing such performances for years. When the manager of the opera house wanted to charge rent for its use, she told him she had never before paid rent for such a thing, which was absolutely true. She talked him out of it. She placed newspaper publicity stories, capitalizing on her background as a graduate of the University of Missouri Journalism School. She unequivocally stated that the principal characters for the Washburn show were "the finest she had ever worked with any place."

With good publicity, hard-working rehearsals, razzle-dazzle, and townwide promotion, she produced a fairly successful show. However, in little Washburn, population under 2,000, "fairly successful" did not quite add up to Raymond's profit requirements.

The sad news surfaced at receipt-counting time. That was when Fran and the sponsors divided all the show proceeds into three piles. The first took care of expenses, which were sharply limited by the contract. The second and third piles were equal cuts of the rest—one-half for the sponsoring organization and one-half for Universal. The second and third piles *had* to equal at least $100 each if Fran was to get another assignment from Universal. In Washburn it looked as if they would until the very last moment, when the printer stalked in and slapped down a bill for $7.00. Fran had not counted on that.

"Couldn't you contribute this work to our worthy cause?" she cajoled. She argued and threatened, but his answer remained a firm no. So the cuts for the Women's Club and Universal were reduced to $96.50 each.

These few dollars were *not* going to stand between Franceswayne Allen and her dream of success. She dug into her purse, found $2 she didn't need, wired her father for $5, and reported to Universal that the cuts were $100 even. Soon a telegram arrived assigning her to her next show. She bought a forty-year career for $7.

# The Stewarts of Iowa
## and How They Made
## Hometown Show Biz Pay

*For good or ill,* Fran's early trouping was to be closely en-
twined with the Stewarts' company. At the time of her graduation in
1928, the talents of these remarkable brothers were little recognized even
in their hometown. A Fairfield banker advised Georgia Seabury (Gould)
of Plainview, Nebr., to exercise caution in her dealings with them when
she enrolled in a smaller, earlier training class. The Stewarts were new in
their business and would bear careful watching, the banker explained.

Yet even then the brothers were on their way to becoming the
Horatio Algers of Fairfield. During a brilliant decade, spanning un-
precedented hard times and depression, their productions would play in
literally thousands of towns, including every one that was county seat size
and larger in the United States and Canada. They would draw audiences
of up to ten million. Their dramatic coaches would direct perhaps a half-
million amateur actors. For a time they would make home talent big-time
show biz.

This was exactly as they planned. Already, in that summer of 1928,
Universal's stationery proclaimed the company the largest in the Middle
West. By the spring of 1929 the brothers had become the self-styled
"world's greatest specialists in amateur productions." "Our sole aim,"
wrote Raymond Stewart, "is to build up the greatest organization of
coaches that the country has ever seen or ever will see." Quite probably
they succeeded.

This, and their personal goal of financial success, would be achieved
by offering attractive opportunities to their show sponsors. "The purpose

of staging Universal shows is to earn money for the sponsoring organizations, build community spirit, give good, clean, wholesome entertainment, and to increase the prestige of the sponsoring organization," stated a Universal training manual.

The Stewarts were born in Fairfield. Their father, the Reverend Samuel S. Stewart, was a pioneer in the Iowa District of the Free Methodist Church. He preached in a number of area churches as an evangelist and brought crowds of up to 7,000 people to camp meetings where "horses and wagons lined the highway . . . for two miles." Even then a Stewart was packing in the crowds.

At an early age the boys learned the value of discipline and hard work when their father's retirement made it necessary for them to contribute to the support of the family.

Most of the thirteen Stewart children graduated from Fairfield High School, five with honors—among these were Raymond and Wilson. Raymond was also a champion debater. He worked his way through almost four years at Grinnell College in Iowa. First he sold candy to theaters, where he got his first whiff of show business. Then he wrote a book, *Stewart's Original System of Candy Making for the Home,* which he personally merchandised. W.T. helped him demonstrate candy cooking in sorority and fraternity houses. Later the younger Merle Stewart helped sell the candy.

"Perhaps the true secret of the brothers' success lies in the fact that each has a deep respect for the ability of the other three," wrote Franceswayne. "Each has his own job but none makes a decision until all are in agreement. Raymond, officially known as the General Manager (there is no president, since the company idea is share and share alike), is a brilliant man. A genius for organizing. A deep thinker with a razor-edged brain which slashes away needless detail."

When aroused to anger he could erupt like a volcano. Fran quoted her landlady as saying that Iowa farmers passing beneath his office window would sometimes hear his fulminations and remark, "It's that oldest of them Stewart brothers layin' down the law again." Yet with family and intimates Raymond was the most "fatherly" of the four.

Wils, W.T., or simply "Stewart," as he was variously known, had been a valedictorian at Fairfield High. He attended Grinnell College briefly but left to conduct Charleston dancing contests. A friend remembers that he and a girl had a vaudeville act.

The other two, Merle and Weston (Pete), "inherited from their pioneer preacher parent a gentleness, steadfastness of purpose . . . patience and an almost unbelievable awe for the older two," in the words of Franceswayne. Neither went to college.

Merle has been described as fun-loving and more a follower than a leader, though he eventually became Universal's public relations man, a competent trainer of coaches, and the head of their New York office.

Within a year of their father's death in 1927, the four Stewarts opened offices over shops at 110 North Main Street, Fairfield. By 1931, according to Orville Prill who joined them that year, they had expanded to include a costume shop and storeroom across the alley. By 1934 they had taken over the entire second floor of what is now Spurgeon's Department Store and had leased a warehouse and costume shop at 112 North Main Street. In the 1930s, they also opened branch offices of varying permanency outside Fairfield.

One key to the company's growth was its detailed intelligence system, which was presided over by Pete. He maintained three large, framed maps dotted with hundreds of varicolored pins. These showed where the company had previously staged plays, where current productions were playing, and where future shows were booked. In August 1930 the *Fairfield Ledger* reported that pins stretched from coast to coast and across the southern provinces of Canada. The thickest pin forests stood in Iowa, Missouri, Illinois, and the rest of the Midwest.

Mazie Lesher (Messer) of rural Fairfield mapped the locations of shows staged by rival home talent companies. To identify such show bookings, she read stacks of clippings of competitive publicity sent to Universal by a bureau. Different colored pins denoted different rivals.

From the maps and other sources Pete determined where to book Universal shows. In later years, according to Prill, they were scheduled only for towns of 3,500 population and larger.

A stenographic staff, which eventually grew to number at least a dozen, was headed by Pete Stewart's wife Helen, who had taken stenography at Fairfield High in preparation for a job with Universal. Like all the company's employees, she pitched in when there were other jobs to be done. She remembers that when the company was short on cash to meet the payroll, she and Merle made candy and sold it around the square in Fairfield on Saturdays after regular working hours.

Besides being the company's cost accountant, Prill was in charge of routing costumes. At first each coach carried those for her show in a trunk furnished by the company. Typical of the Stewarts' determination to leave nothing to chance, Prill remembers that they tested one trunk by throwing it from a two-story building and then turning a hose on it for several days. It withstood both ordeals.

Later, when the costumes became more elaborate and abundant, they were shipped directly to show sites. Well-coordinated organization and timing was required. Because of such scheduling pressure, it was only with great difficulty that Prill wrangled permission to attend his first wife's funeral.

Stewart productions used virtually no props or scenery that could not be found everywhere, such as the pile of potatoes around which the action revolved in their second play, *Corporal Eagen.* For scenic background, the audience had to rely on its imagination.

Raymond managed the bookers, or salespeople, who numbered forty to fifty at the height of operations in the early 1930s. Ethel Van Hon (Garretson) became one of the company's rare female bookers in the summer of 1928. A booker's career, she recalled, began with several weeks of classes running from eight in the morning to ten in the evening. Raymond, sometimes assisted by W.T., instructed the bookers by performing as recalcitrant prospects to condition them to overcome the most difficult objections. Raymond, as an ex-debater, would explain how both a debater and a booker had to anticipate every possible argument the prospect might raise and to have a good rebuttal ready.

Raymond then sent the bookers out on two-week schedules and told them "not to leave a town that wasn't booked." Normally it took no more than a day to book a town. In the last scheduled town, the booker received mail, another list of towns, and pay but received nothing in the interim. When bookers, according to Ethel, arrived on location, they went first to the newspaper office where they learned the identities of the most prominent local people.

The outstanding booker was L. K. Woods, who worked primarily in New England. One season he booked 143 shows—more than twice that of any other Universal booker. He was said to have been able to sign anyone. The fabulous promises he (and his colleagues) made to sign some shows caused many coaches to curse bookers silently as they struggled to resell the contract. But coaches had reason to bless Woods, too. When there weren't enough bookings to keep them all working, the Stewarts would send L.K. to the rescue, and shortly there would be work for all.

# ᑐ 7 ᑐ

# The Coach's
# Daily Procedure

*Fran may have been* on her own, but this did not mean that
she was away from the Stewarts' control. They held nearly absolute rein
over field activities through a daily procedure regimen that the coaches
learned from a manual adapted to each show.

Fran Allen described the daily procedure directives for the Stewarts'
first production as "eighty-five typewritten pages detailing the work
every hour for sixteen hours a day while the girl is in the town." This may
be an exaggeration, but not by much. The coach was required to promise
at her opening committee meeting: "Remember, I am at your sevice from
five in the morning to midnight." Ila Claussen (Rix) of Manning, Iowa,
remembered that many a night she simply flopped on her bed too exhausted to change to nightwear.

Like a juggler keeping seven balls in the air, the coach had to perform
seven separate jobs: sign up the cast; direct the show; take care of
finances; attend to tickets and reservations; do the advertising and promotion; check in, assign, and ship out costumes and other properties; and
handle contact with the sponsoring organization in such a way as to create
perpetual goodwill with it and the town.

A typical coach entered her town on a Monday morning. "On arrival,
we must locate and meet with the president of the sponsoring organization," Fran wrote in summarizing the manual. "At this meeting we
should inquire about 'a good place to stay,' request a committee meeting
in two or three hours, and not neglect to praise both the town and the person who has greeted us."

The coach requested that her contact take her to the meeting, dropping by the newspaper office on the way. The coach would want to be introduced to the editor, "get lined up on our advertising," and arrange for daily stories in the paper.

Margarete Morse wrote that W.T. told them "to go into the dirtiest, most disarrayed newspaper office and turn on the charm—'glow' is the word I've coined for the approach—and look at just everything, scrutinize with joy, pick up different pieces of type and ask questions, almost embrace the linotype, and even try to help staff set type by hand! Go to see newspaper folks every day. If the editor will talk, engage him in conversation. Make a friend of the big shot, but do not fail to notice and be charming to all. Help the janitor, if needed."

In early afternoon the coach conducted her first committee meeting. She delivered a speech, tailor-made for building confidence. Then she asked for the names of the twenty most prominent business and professional people in town. She directed the committee in selecting the cast, making sure it included those people.

The director also helped the committee set the price of admission and choose locations for rehearsals, headquarters, ticket reservations, and an overhead across-the-street sign. She found the names and meeting times of the town's civic organizations so that she could talk to as many as possible. She learned the name of the auditorium manager so that she could double-check her information about rental, seating capacity, and stock tickets.

The coach and committee then chose several people to help distribute tickets; several others to help with costumes; and still others to work with props, the children in the Baby Pageant, posters, and so on. The general chairman would assist with the main advertising. Boys were chosen to act as captains over other boys who would distribute publicity.

When this rigorous meeting adjourned, the coach turned to signing up the cast. "We never ask anybody to be in the show," Fran emphasized. "We tell them the committee has chosen them to be in it." If someone were merely asked, it would be too easy to refuse. But being honored as the choice of fellow citizens was a different matter. Surprisingly, Universal coaches had very few rejections.

The director might wind up her first day by selling a few ads for the handbill or by putting some stickers on cars. After that she made out her daily report, informing the Stewarts what had been done that day, how many people had agreed to be in the show and their positions in the community, the number of seats that would be put on reserve, the number of people working on the show, the atmosphere of the town, the attitude toward the coach and show, and so on. This came easily for Fran, a voluminous letter writer.

The daily procedure continued unrelentingly through the week, piling detail upon detail, deadline for performing each duty upon deadline. Saturday, when the director specifically was warned against leaving town, was plaster day and the town was to be literally plastered with advertising. A coach might stage a parade if weather permitted. The daily procedure told her how to go about it. She placed cards in every store window, cards or posters on the light posts, stickers on all the cars in sight, and had her over-the-street sign flapping in a prominent location. Boys distributed handbills that carried programs of the show on one side and advertising from town merchants on the other.

On Sunday morning a coach was free to attend church, the daily procedure advised. Previously she would have tried to arrange for "all the churches and Sunday schools in the town" to announce the show in some way, whether from bulletin board or pulpit. On Sunday afternoon she might conduct a rehearsal if any of the cast needed special help. Should there be a movie or other public entertainment, she would stand outside distributing handbills. Any extra time would be devoted to marking her reserved tickets and getting the seating plat ready for ticket sales.

A more hectic pace started again on Monday, building to the climax, which was the two nights of performance. These were scheduled on Wednesday, Thursday, Friday, or Saturday, depending on local circumstances. The financial accounting immediately followed the last show. Cleanup duties occupied the next day, and by the weekend all a coach had to be concerned about was getting on to her next town.

In addition to the daily procedure, the Stewarts laid down rules of personal behavior for coaches. The guidelines were imprinted so firmly in the mind of former coach Ernestine Hoffman (Smith) of Elk Point, S. Dak., that she remembered them after half a century:

1. Stay in whatever room they pick for you and pretend you like it.
2. Don't date.
3. Don't smoke unless you flush the stub down the toilet.
4. Always say everything is going beautifully; everyone is cooperating.
5. "You'll love your show."
6. Don't ever kick anyone out of the cast no matter that they can't speak out, can't keep time, drink too much, or whatever.
7. If you do everything we tell you, when we tell you, all will go well. You'll have a smash.
8. Change clothes three times a day even if you have only three outfits.
9. The more children you get in the opening pageant, the better your crowd will be. Everyone comes to see their kids.

That Universal's training and hour-by-hour regimentation proved effective is testified to by almost all coaches. They had a lifetime impact on many. "We knew exactly what to do from the time we entered a town to the time we left it," wrote former coach Georgia Drexler (Durr) of Yachats, Oreg. "We were the best trained people in the U.S.! I never had such marvelous training in anything before or since." Evelyn Thompson of Lake City, Iowa, who later worked for another home talent producer commented, "The training I had with Universal was unquestionably the better."

The impression on customer organizations also tended to be favorable, as evidenced by hundreds of testimonial letters. To quote one from Austin, Tex., of March, 1930, "At first we thought it was absolutely impossible. . . . I am still wondering how it was done. One merchant here told me he thought it was the best thing ever done in our city to get a feeling of good fellowship among all the businesspeople."

Such, then, were the results achieved by the Stewarts' woman coaches. On the hometown firing lines they won the battle of making show business pay for Universal.

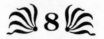

# ≫ 8 ≪

# Aunt Lucia,
## All-Time Hit of the American Stage

*The instant* she stepped onstage—or was shoved on from the wings—she was a hit. The audience couldn't help laughing. Her outsized gray wig kept slipping over her head and face. Her black two-piece dress simply wouldn't stay together right. She was incredibly awkward, but she had to cavort athletically while trying to elude men who wanted to marry her for her money.

The best part of the joke was that the "she" was not only a he, but that he was also one of the best-known men of the town, who was making a fool of himself to the delight of his fellow citizens.

He was the lead character of *Aunt Lucia,* a play that local newspapers described variously as a musical farce, a great collegiate comedy, the best home talent show ever seen in the town, frivolous, hilarious, screamingly funny. Almost invariably hometown reviewers spoke of it in glowing terms. This explains why *Aunt Lucia* played in virtually every town that was of county seat size or larger in the United States and Canada, a record probably unequaled by any other theatrical production. It is highly likely that more people saw this play than any of the major long-run hits that have appeared on New York's Broadway stages. In brief, *Aunt Lucia* can lay claim to being one of the all-time hits of the American amateur stage.

*Aunt Lucia* was the Stewart brothers' first trump card, and they built their organization on it. The unlikely playwright was Raymond Stewart, with an assist from Wilson, who drew on his Charleston show background. The result was a slapstick comedy interspersed with dancing and musical numbers, devised strictly for amateur casts.

The Stewarts began their home talent careers by personally staging *Aunt Lucia,* after engaging one or more girls to help direct it. Mary Williams (Nordstrom) of Burlington, Iowa, assisted Wilson when the play premiered in Fairfield on September 29, 1927. The *Fairfield Ledger* reported that the play had "been staged in towns all over Iowa and Missouri in the past two years and has played to packed houses everywhere." It was this favorable reception that encouraged the brothers to form Universal Producing Company.

*Aunt Lucia* was described by Fran as "a three-act comedy, which the Stewarts have repeatedly told us is NOT a steal from *Charley's Aunt.* But since I know that show so well and Charley's Aunt 'is from Brazil, where the nuts come from' (a line used in this script, too), methinks the boys do protest too much."

Certainly there is a strong resemblance to *Charley's Aunt,* but the plot of *Aunt Lucia* is less sophisticated, with more horseplay and comic routines, dances, and songs than its British alleged prototype.

The action occured in a fraternity living room during homecoming week at Bula Bula College. The wealthy, widowed aunt of one of the fraternity brothers was to visit the campus and would, they all hoped, contribute a half-million dollars for a new football stadium. The boys also hoped that she would chaperone so they could entertain their girl friends at the house. Two elderly characters, a butter-and-egg man and a professor, had other hopes—to gain Aunt Lucia's hand and fortune in marriage. When the real Aunt Lucia's visit was delayed, one of the fraternity boys, Jerry, was conned into impersonating the old lady with predictably funny results. The fake Aunt Lucia's antics in avoiding her suitors and in chaperoning progressed from one slapstick gag to another. The arrival of the real Aunt Lucia, disguised and escorted by Jerry's girl friend, brought the show to its comic climax.

Specialty numbers were introduced throughout. These gave the show sparkle and provided for almost unlimited participation by townsfolk. Up to 50 people took part in these numbers, with some casts totaling 200, 300, and even 500.

As one of Fran's letters described them: "First come the children in the curtain raiser, called 'Take Me Back to Babyland,' in which nearly every youngster in town from grades one through four is invited to take part. The idea is that each child will automatically bring an average of eight mammas, papas, and grandparents to see them or at least to take them home; either way they have to have a ticket. The children appear on stage clad in sleepwear and sit or lie enrapt while a woman gives a dramatic reading to them."

The Collegiate Chorus appeared immediately afterward. It was composed of fifteen or more of the best singers among the town's businesspeople, or was a locally favorite choir or choral group. They would be "dressed in sweaters, knickers, and general college styles." In later productions they also wore matching caps and carried bright, colored pennants and canes. They sang "Hail, Hail, the Gang's All Here," "Bula, Bula," "Collegiate," and one or two other college pep numbers to set the homecoming week mood.

Between acts the third special group appeared. This was recruited from the town's popular teenage girls who "wear white sailor pants and sing 'Breezing Along with the Breeze,' " according to Fran. "In another number they wear their own evening dresses and do a dance routine and song to 'In an Old Fashioned Garden.' " Later the company furnished farmerette costumes for the second number, in which the girls sang "Out in the New Mown Hay" and "Dew, Dew, Dewy Day." In 1929 Pauline Fossler (Wilkinson) introduced a "Singing in the Rain" routine, which she taught to the other *Aunt Lucia* coaches at the summer 1929 convention. "The costumes," Pauline explained, "were easily found in the girls' wardrobes: slickers, rain hats, and galoshes. Before their entrance, I watered them with a sprinkling can."

But the real crowd-swelling group was the Flapper Chorus that appeared in act two. Selected for this odd honor were, if possible, the mayor, the chief of police, doctors, dentists, lawyers, educators, leading businessmen, and politicians. If the coach could sign up the town's most popular male (in at least one instance it was the undertaker), she had no trouble getting the others. All impersonated college girls. A "red-headed freshman" introduced them with "Now, ladies and gentlemen, your evening's entertainment would not be complete unless you met the flapper girls of our college. They are very shy and bashful, but I believe I can get them out here if I do a little coaxing. They are all members of that famous coed organization of Bula Bula College, the Sig-a-Sig-a-Rette sorority. I will now introduce each and every one for your approval."

The orchestra played and the chorus entered, dancing and singing "Who's That Pretty Baby?"

> Ain't she pretty, ain't she sweet,
> Just the kind you'd like to meet.
> Who's that pretty baby?
> Pearly teeth and pretty hair
> Rolls her own and she don't care.
> Who's that pretty baby?

The singers were bedecked with mops for wigs, Clara Bow lips, short skirts, bathing suits, long johns, hairy legs, fluffy ballet skirts, balloon bosoms, stilts, and hundreds of other costuming and makeup gimmicks.

One by one they broke from the chorus line and pranced around the stage. They impersonated the sorority president, the gold digger, the girl about town, the clinging vine, the innocent freshman, the campus flirt, the studious girl, the most popular, the conceited junior, the peppiest, the baby-face, dancing girls, or stage stars. Among the latter might be travesties of Gloria Swanson, Clara Bow, Greta Garbo, Norma Shearer, Pola Negri, Theda Bara, Colleen Moore, Louise Fazenda, Bebe Daniels, or Lila Lee. Also prevalent were Tillie the Toiler, Winnie Winkle, Orphan Annie, Jiggs's Maggie, and other funny paper characters. They always raised a roar of laughter.

Sometimes specialty numbers would be added to accommodate local talent. Grace Barrington (Hofer) remembers a young man in her show in Santa Cruz, Calif., who did Salome's dance of the seven veils. In another of her towns, the flappers passed a prop set of false teeth back and forth. Still elsewhere, Grace's flappers went "around a maypole to the tune of 'Chicken Reel.' " In Alameda, Calif., they appeared in a Paramount Films newsreel that was shown all over the country.

An *Aunt Lucia* script, ragged from hard use, survives as the possession of former coach Thelma Bump (Duesenberg). Its fourteen coverless, single spaced, dimly mimeographed pages embody the essence of Universal's successful home talent formula. The speeches are short and snappy, the situations easy to grasp, the roles many—eighteen parts in the play and an almost unlimited number in the specialties. The play offered rudimentary situation comedy, intensified with music and dancing, and the opportunity to dress up or to laugh at those that did.

The Stewarts did not stop there. They made sure that when *Aunt Lucia* entered a town, her coming was no secret. By 1928, they had become masters of publicity, and they grew in this capability as their imaginative coaches fed them new angles.

Besides the posters, handbills, car stickers, advertising, and street banner, the coaches were encouraged to develop unusual publicity gimmicks. In one town Fran wrote a series of columns headed "Down the Line with *Aunt Lucia*," which took the form of amusing interviews with the various local actors and their experiences with their parts. In Rensselaer, Ind., the editor of the local paper had a crush on director Evelyn Thompson, so daily he wrote something silly mentioning her and the show. He'd make up little quips like:

> Fish in the ocean, soup in the sea
> A red-haired director
> Made a sap out of me.

The coaches also used pictorial material in the papers. The Stewarts supplied cartoon drawings of the cast principals. Sometimes there would be pictures of the coach, of the leads in the show, or of the *Aunt Lucia* specialty groups in costume at rehearsal. In Springfield, Mo., Fran added face shots of the leading businessmen in her Flapper Chorus to pictures of the bodies of bathing beauties for eye-catching publicity.

The coaches also used radio. Pauline Fossler, a singer as well as a coach, tried to negotiate a radio appearance wherever there was a local station. She also arranged to sing a solo in a local church. "Usually this was possible," she said. "This helped in two ways: it kept me in practice and netted a bit of advertising for the show."

Even the telephone became an advertising tool. One coach remembers that the Stewarts told her to give the operator free tickets to the show. The hope was that she would say, "Don't miss *Aunt Lucia* while she's in town!" when she was putting through calls.

Other promotions were kiddie matinees and parades. The former gave the *Aunt Lucia* cast a dress rehearsal before a live audience. It was held after school, and children were usually admitted for a dime. Parades were comprised of anything that moved and could be enlisted, from small processions of new cars, the local fire truck, and open cars or trucks holding costumed actors to more elaborate ones with marching bands and floats.

By the fall of 1930, Universal's *Big Black Book* appeared for all coaches to carry. It was full of letters of recommendation, newspaper articles, pictures, and other material showing the scope and importance of the company and its *Aunt Lucia* production. The *Black Book* doubled as a scrapbook for the individual girls, who would affix their own letters of recommendation, clippings, and pictures.

The promotional enthusiasm of the coaches was whipped to a high pitch by the *Bulletin*s sent to them regularly. Whenever the Stewarts heard of a new way to advertise their play, the *Bulletin*s spread the word. A slick newspaper, *The Universal News,* was also issued with success stories about the top coaches and bookers. Fran often contributed.

The Stewarts staged contests to urge coaches to greater money-making zeal. Prizes ranged from imitation gold cups to five-dollar gold pieces, stockings, or costume jewelry.

Through 1928, 1929, and 1930, the appeal of *Aunt Lucia* and the force of all-out promotion behind it helped build the Stewarts' operations. The brothers declared 1930 their "Whoopee Year." Never mind the Great Depression. "While other businesses talked of it," trumpeted the *Bulletin,* "Universal made Whoopee." Another group of coaches began doing *Corporal Eagen* in 1929, which also helped the process.

Meanwhile, time had begun to run out for the dear old lady who had helped make all this possible. Having played coast to coast to the laughter and applause of almost every possible hometown audience, *Aunt Lucia* was ready to retire. A January 1931 *Bulletin* announced that starting January 19 the *Aunt Lucia* group of coaches were to do another play, *College Flapper.*

Thus ended the career of a not-to-be-forgotten star of the American home talent circuit. Her success had started rumors among the other traveling theater companies that the Stewarts were making a million dollars a year. This could have been an exaggeration, but it did highlight the fact that, awkward and ugly as Aunt Lucia always was, she had worked something of a financial miracle for Universal and for the business reputation of home talent shows. Even if she was always a he, she was quite a girl!

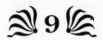

# Pilgrims
# of the Impossible

*Universal coaches* soon learned that no daily procedure or training adequately prepared them for all the realities of the road. Their nerve, resourcefulness, and bulldog determination would prove the ultimate requirement for making hometown show biz pay.

Of this the Stewarts were well aware, and they spared no pains to inspire in their directors an evangelistic fervor that would sustain them through their trials. Universal coaches, they exhorted, were invincible. They gave them as a rallying cry the brainchild of coach Isabel Jane Fry: "Universal coaches are pilgrims of the impossible."

Further, each girl, at least at one point in Universal's history, was supplied with a copy of Kipling's "If," which begins:

> If you can keep your head when all about you
> Are losing theirs and blaming it on you. . . .

On the road this inspiration was sorely needed. "Coaching," former coach Grace Barrington remembers, "was a grueling, exhausting, sometimes thankless job. Our days were long and hard." Opal Jester (Morgan) of Tulsa, Okla., recalls fainting at one of her dress rehearsals, the result of combined exhaustion and frostbite suffered while putting stickers on cars. Many girls quit because of nearly total debility or illness.

There were nightmarish times when everything during a production went wrong. In Fran's show in Franklin, Tenn., in the spring of 1929, the actor playing Aunt Lucia lost his wig in his most important scene. The whiskers of the old professor came off while he did his dance. A chorus girl kicked off her slipper into the center section of the audience. A patron caught it and attempted to throw it back, hitting the piano player on the head. The butter-and-egg man, portrayed by the headmaster of an exclusive boys' school, ripped the rear seam of his pants when he knelt to propose.

Meanwhile, the students from his school got into the costume trunk and swiped the pennants and caps of the Collegiate Chorus. Next they invaded the dressing room of the high school chorus girls and tied the clothes there in hard knots. The girls' mothers wouldn't let them come back the next night, so instead of a chorus line, Fran had two girls do each chorus number. "Nuts!" she concluded in disgust. Still, the townfolk said the pranks were "all in fun and it was a swell show."

Small-town electric service was often primitive, not infrequently plunging theaters into darkness in the middle of a production. "What's happened? Do something!" Fran shouted at a tough old stagehand when this occurred in O'Fallon, Ill., in February 1929.

"Goddamned transformer over on Cherry street has just burned out," he answered.

"Well, don't just stand there like a ninny. Do something," Fran repeated.

The man lit a match, spit a stream of tobacco barely missing her silver shoes, and yelled, " 'Do somethin'. Do somethin'.' Wal, Jesus Christ, lady, who do you think I am? I told you the transformer went out and not even God Almighty kin fix that 'til they get a 'lectrician from the power plant up a pole."

Fran sent for a gross of candles from a nearby drugstore. "We put these out on the stage apron, and the characters went through the third act by candlelight. Then in time for the finale, all stage lights went up."

Universal's promotional practices often led to confrontations with local citizens. Coach Billie Cook (Roth) from Jefferson City, Mo., was caught pasting stickers on cars. The authorities ordered her to scrape them off, which would require precious hours she couldn't spare. Billie's solution was to put a notice in the paper informing all motorists who wanted the stickers removed to show up at a designated gas station. There she had teenage girls from the cast, resplendent in their show costumes, remove the offending ads with razor blades.

In late February 1929 in Paragould, Ark., firemen, who could usually be counted on to hang the overhead banner, refused to raise Fran's. "Everyone kept complaining it was too much trouble," Fran wrote, "until I said, 'Shucks, I can climb those telephone poles myself. You act like a bunch of sissies.' " The mayor came to her rescue with a dare. "If you climb one pole, I'll climb the other." "So I got up one pole and his honor up the other," Fran wrote. "Unbeknownst to him I had a photographer there, and he took a picture, which appeared in the local sheet under the caption, '*Aunt Lucia* Has the Mayor Up in the Air.' Sold out and made one of the biggest cuts of the season."

Cast dropouts, feuding, and actor recalcitrance caused recurring problems. In Mt. Pulaski, Ill., Fran's second town in the fall of 1928, she applied a drastic remedy to such a case. The most popular man in town had been chosen to play Aunt Lucia. He had a moustache and had promised to shave it. But on the night of the show he appeared still wearing it. His girl, he explained, had told him she wouldn't go out with him if he shaved it, and he would not sacrifice it. "I'll cover it with adhesive tape," he said, "or some kind of makeup."

Fran thought this would certainly ruin the credibility of Aunt Lucia. She "got two fellows from the American Legion," sponsors of the show, "to grab him and hold him down while the local barber shaved the moustache." He swore he'd walk out. The cue for his entrance came; he was still arguing. He had on his costume and was standing with his back to the stage, so Fran gave him a shove. "He made a backward, flying-tackle type of entrance that brought down the house. Afterwards I always used it as part of the show." His girl liked him better without the moustache; Fran received a wire from them two weeks after she left town announcing their marriage.

A messy cast controversy almost put a show coached by Grace Barrington out of business in a Wisconsin town. There Grace made a special effort to sign up two women from the Rabinski family (not their real name) who "owned practically everything in town." One had been a prostitute and wouldn't allow her first name on the program. Further, because of her participation two cast members quit. One Rabinski was assigned a good part, but the other was infuriated when given a minor role. After threatening to "knock Grace through the wall," she dropped out. Then, on the grounds that "we Rabinskis always stick together," the other sister quit too. The committee chairman insisted on getting them back because they owned the theater, the rehearsal hall, and the only spotlight in town, and they had promised to donate them all. The chairman and Grace spent an entire evening before finally persuading them both to return.

Fran learned two good lessons from one cast problem. She had "a perfectly terrible actor" playing the lead in *Aunt Lucia*. She sounded off about how "dumb, homely, and awful" he was to another cast member, who replied, "Well, Miss Allen, he is my first cousin." Fran apologized and tucked away the lesson—never criticize a cast member to any other local. To avoid more offense, she used the man anyway. After the show she was amazed when "about fifty people" came to her to say, "Boy, oh boy, wasn't Tom good as the lead. He's a real natural-born actor. I'll bet you wish you could take him along and have him in every one of your shows, don't you?"

The experience taught her "the most important secret for the success of amateur show business," Fran decided. "Every town and community thinks their own people are better than anyone else in the world. You soon lose any illusion that you need a particular type of man to play a certain part. He can be too big, too little, too fat, too skinny, red, gray, or bald-headed, just so long as he is well known and well liked locally. If so, he'll be the star of the show, no matter what the director thinks."

In one of Jewell T. Wilson's casts a feud broke out among actors, and several days before the show six people quit. Jewell, who was one of Universal's top money-makers, called on Billie Cook, who was coaching in a nearby town, for help. Billie telegraphed the Stewarts that she couldn't get an auditorium, would do her show a week later, and responded to Jewell's call.

The two coaches trained one replacement, and between them they took the five remaining parts. Billie opened the show with an introductory dramatic reading in which she portrayed an army captain, even though she was wearing a skirt. She didn't have time to change before handling her other roles and told the audience they'd have to use their imaginations. Billie also did two women characters in the play. To avoid their appearing on the stage together as called for in the script, she had to do considerable ad-libbing.

Fire protection regulations were lax or nonexistent at auditoriums in some small towns. In Union City, Tenn., on May 2, 1929, Fran had "one of the most terrible experiences of my career. The first night of the show, after I got the children onstage for the Baby Pageant, I said to a stagehand, 'I smell something burning, don't you?' He sniffed and said, 'Yeah, I smell something kinda hot too. He located a 300-watt bulb resting against the rung of a stepladder, which had caused the wood to blacken and smoke, and turned it off."

She still kept smelling smoke and told him so. "Nuts. You're just nervous and excited."

"I am not," Fran told him. "There is something on fire here, and with 130 kids on stage, I'm worried. Please go down to the basement, out in the alley, and everywhere to see if you can find it. Don't let on because it will cause a panic, and these kids will be trampled to death."

He was back soon looking white as a sheet. "Dressin' room under the stage is on fire, but I got a fire extinguisher, and the floor's concrete and the walls are tile. I can handle it—I think."

"I was positively shaking all over," Fran remembered, "but I had to keep smiling at those little kids out there on the stage who looked at me with big, trusting, saucerlike eyes. All the time I thought, I've got to get them off that stage, the fire is right under them. But it will be only a couple of minutes until the number is over. Then if I don't scare them, they'll do what I tell them. I don't believe I ever prayed so hard. When the curtain went down, I went out on the stage and said, 'All right, put your fingers to your lips and follow me,' and I led them off the stage and out the back door into the alley."

By this time smoke had come up and was filling the entire back of the stage. The older people in the cast were running around, saying "I smell smoke, there must be a fire. Is there a fire, Miss Allen?"

She answered, "You know this theater is fireproof. It's just somebody burning trash."

The stagehand came up and said, "It's okay."

Fran said, "Are you sure?"

He replied, "Sure. Just some paper and trash. Nothing to it. But if I was you, I would go out and make an announcement to the audience, because when you pull the curtain, they are going to see the smoke."

Fran went before the curtain and said, "Ladies and gentlemen, pardon me for interrupting the show, but it seems trash and old papers were being burned, and when we turned on the ventilators in the theater, we noticed it smelled like something burning in here. However, this is not true. There is no fire. I am making this announcement because there are parents who had children in the opening number, and I didn't want you to worry. They are out of the building, and chaperones are taking them over to the recreation center for an ice cream treat. There is no danger, but as a safety measure I have made this announcement because I did not want anyone to get panicky if they smelled smoke."

Fran went on with the show. Meanwhile the stagehand confided that the entire dressing room under the stage had been gutted—that is, the wooden boards used as makeup tables around the walls had burned.

"The funny thing," Fran recalled, "was the reaction of half the cast. Instead of thinking the stagehand and I had done something heroic, they were furious and said we had taken their lives into our hands by going on with the show. The next night a fireman came around to stand backstage, a case of locking the barn door after the horse was gone. He said to me, 'Lady, we sure want to congratulate you on using your head, keeping cool and handling this thing the way you did. It could have been serious if people had started a stampede.' Like a sissy I broke down and cried. He said, 'If that's not just like a woman, crying twenty-four hours too late.' "

Fire played a role in others of Fran's road experiences. Early in May

1929 in Tullahoma, Tenn., Fran first used fire to her advantage. She staged a parade with all her chorus girls on the fire truck. About the time the parade was over, the siren sounded, but she told the girls to hang on. The truck charged off to a false alarm, and Fran had further advertised the show.

Six days later, however, she became the victim of a real fire. The hotel in which she was staying caught fire at night. Fran climbed down a rope to the roof over the front porch and down a ladder, but all she brought with her were her lucky shoes. The woman who owned the hotel went into the guest rooms, threw clothes out of the closets onto the bed covers and then dropped these out of the windows. The guests lost very little, although the two upper stories of the hotel were demolished. Fran's costume trunks were burned badly on the outside and saturated with water, but the costumes inside were safe. The Stewarts' testing had paid off.

Epidemics also confronted the coaches. A flu epidemic swept an Illinois town as Fran's show was nearing production in December 1928. A health officer told her she would have to cancel. Fran, however, already had a $250 advance sale on tickets, and she knew that even if none were sold at the door, she and Universal would make money. She ignored the order to close and proceeded to play the show even though the authorities ran a story on the front page of the local paper advising everyone to stay out of crowds. This was positioned next to Fran's plug about *Aunt Lucia.*

On the show nights, only $10 worth of door tickets were sold. Not even 50 people came to either production. Yet, since the program advertising had taken care of expenses, Universal made a cut of $130. This experience drove home to Fran W.T.'s philosophy "advance ticket sales mean health, accident, and welfare insurance in the Stewarts' home talent business."

Wilson Stewart told his coaches that if they could handle the job for six months, they could do anything. Problems with sponsoring committees were another coaching trouble that supported his statement. Fran knew this from a pre-Universal experience in 1926 with the ill-fated Associated Producers. The committee in Elwood, Ind., had thought from her name that she was a man. On her arrival, they decided to wire her company that they would not accept a woman because the director had to build a stage in the armory. Fran told them she had built a stage in every town, but they still sent the wire. The company wired back to let her start the show, and they'd send a man to replace her. After five days Fran had won over the chairwoman, who asked her to stay. Fran did not know a 2 × 4 board from a shingle or even that lumber came in dimensions, but she solved that problem by talking the local National Guard unit into erecting the stage for her. She ended with a magnificent 20- by 40-foot stage capable of supporting 150 people and equipped with colored lights.

That didn't end the Elwood experience. Fran programmed a big flashlight chorus there. "This takes care of all the buck-toothed, cross-eyed, fat, or lean and lanky girls in the chorus," she explained. "They are told this is to be a very unusual number with special lighting effects. Until the night of the show they did not realize that all the lights are turned out on the number, as the girls swing flashlights in their hands in small or large circles, singing 'I Think I See Your Face Out There.' If they are out of step it doesn't matter. Their names are on the program and their families are in the audience." During the number, one girl danced off the stage apron in the darkness. She landed on the bass drum, breaking its head and injuring her legs. There was some talk of suing the sponsoring organization and the company, but the cast took up a collection and sent the girl a bouquet. Fran sent a potted plant. The doctor sent bills to the producing company for a couple of months, which were ignored until he gave up.

A different type of sponsoring problem occurred when coach Billie Cook arrived in a town in the dead of a cold, snowy winter. After considerable searching, she located her club president in shantytown. The impoverished, elderly woman confessed she had done nothing about the show because of the cold weather and because she had no phone or car. Billie called on other club members, finding them all elderly, ill, or unable to shoulder the show's demands. Back in the lobby of her hotel, more determined than ever to somehow put on her show, Billie fell into conversation with a hotel resident, a local lawyer. Soon she had him so interested that he and some friends formed a committee to conduct the event. They told Billie that they wanted to help since the old women wanted so much to do something for charity.

Emily Stuart Neville had a trying experience when she called the house of the president of her sponsoring Ladies Aid Society. "Someone answered the phone, and said she was down at the church and I couldn't see her," Emily reported. Her reaction was to visit the church.

"What in the world are you doing here?" the president demanded when Emily introduced herself. "We canceled the show last week, because we didn't need the money. And, besides, it is impossible to have it."

Impossible? Emily's heart sank, but she remembered that she was a pilgrim of the impossible. The Ladies Aid was having its weekly lunch. She asked if she might take a plate. She ate and talked and praised the food, the people, the church, the town, and the hills for what seemed an endless time. Casually she brought the conversation back to the show suggesting that they put it on for charity.

"Will you tell me just how much your company gives for charity?" a visiting preacher's wife asked. Someone had done a Universal show in her town but hadn't given her husband's church any of the proceeds. Emily kept her head and patiently explained that the Stewarts were splendid Christian gentlemen, sons of a minister and gave generously to all kinds of charities, a statement she hoped was true.

The ladies weren't convinced. Emily finished her lunch and walked into the kitchen with them to wash dishes. As she washed, she talked to them and cussed to herself. She prayed with the ladies until five o'clock, by which time she had sold them on the show.

At least one natural catastrophe was also likely to be on the schedule of a long-term Universal coach. Fran met hers—a flood—on June 13, 1929, in McMinville, Tenn. High water there had made residents question whether anyone could attend her show, but Fran doggedly prepared for it. The stage was in a school building where the roof was being repaired during vacation time. On show night a cloudburst fell thirty minutes before curtain time. The roofers had covered their work area with a tarpaulin, but this broke. The room where Fran had gathered the children for the Baby Pageant was flooded. Most of the little actors were dressed in nightgowns and pajamas. "Naturally they set up a big howl in nine different keys," Fran commented. The only dry place she could find was the basement under the stage. She herded them down and went on with cast makeup. Ten minutes later the lights in the building went out, and the kids sent up "screams and screeches and groans that sounded like they were victims in the torture dungeons of the Spanish Inquisition."

With the aid of a flashlight Fran picked her way to them. Fran's own words vividly describe the rest of the "McMinville experience":

Those little devils had found how to get into the coal bin, and they had been having a high time throwing coal at each other. The nightgowns and pajamas were stained and streaked. I was so mad I lost my head; and, instead of reassuring them, because naturally they were all petrified down in that black hole, I lit into them. "Look at you. I'd be ashamed. I've got a good notion not to let any of you be in the show. I ought to paddle the lot of you and send you home this very minute."

A couple of them began to whimper and sniffle, and if you have ever managed a bunch of children you know that if one begins to cry, it is as contagious as smallpox. I'd stood as much as I could anyhow, so I yelled at the top of my lungs, "Now stop it! Not another tear, not a whimper. Those of you that are good, I'll send someone down to get you and take you up on the stage, and we'll have a good time playing actors. But the next one that cries will have to stay in the cellar, and I hope the lightning and thunder strike you." Lordy, wasn't that an awful thing to say! When I look back I am surprised that the good Lord Almighty didn't send a thunderbolt down in my direction.

I got the men in the cast to roll up their white duck pants and wade through the water in the flooded dressing room off stage and go down in the basement and bring the children up to the stage. Most men had a youngster under each arm, as the kids were nearly all between six and nine. They put them on the stage, and I went around with a wet towel and wiped off as much coal dust and soot as I could in the few minutes before curtain.

The woman who was supposed to be the "Tell-Me-a-Story-Lady" and do the reading with these children as background failed to show up. I held the curtain about fifteen minutes hoping the rain would let up and she might make it. She failed to show, so I tore off my makeup smock and skinned into an evening dress and prepared to take her place. I walked out to the center of the stage and motioned for all the children to fold their hands, put their heads on them and close their eyes as if they were asleep. Stifled sniffles sounded throughout the group, and I said, "Now, now, nobody must cry. Pretend you are asleep. Curtain."

The spotlight hit me as I took center stage. All seemed to go well through the first verse of "Take Me Back to Babyland." Then I got to the chorus which goes:

> *Take me back to Babyland*
> *Please don't let me grow.*
> *Take me back where Santa Claus*
> *Comes riding through the snow.*

On this line the stagehand gave a shove to the midget Santa Claus bedecked with big flowing whiskers and sitting in a red wagon, and he came sailing out to center stage right on cue. The song continues:

> *Tell again of Cinderella*

calling for the entrance of a little curly-haired cherub dressed in spangles. The cherub entered wearing the spangles but also an enormous pout, her eyes suspiciously red and with a big streak of coal dust across her cheek. But I kept on with the next line.

> *And her prince so grand.*

But no prince appeared, so I repeated the line.

> *And her prince so grand.*

No response. Apprehensive but still smiling wanly at the audience, I took what I hoped were a few graceful steps toward the left wing and shouted,

> AH, YES, AND HER PRINCE SO GRAND.

Behind the heavy velveteen curtain I spied his royal highness, with his cape hanging in front of him like a burlap sack, his ostrich plume drooping across a face that was streaked, sweaty, and puckered into a perplexed frown. He was shaking his head vigorously at me and calling in a stage whisper, "No ma'am, I can't go out there, not right now." Disregarding this plea, I repeated for a fourth time:

*And her prince so grand.*

Reaching into the wings, I grabbed the youngster by the shoulder and yanked him onto the stage in full view of the audience. Then I took a deep breath, faced the spot with my most flashing, maternal smile, and continued:

*Let me be a child like these*
*Back in Babyland.*

These lines were greeted by snickers, then a guffaw or two, and finally uncontrollable laughter—I mean belly laughter—from the audience. I thought perhaps I was losing my petticoat, for by the tone of the laughs the audience was laughing at the act, not with it. Then I looked at the prince. To my horror, instead of holding a stick horse as he had been trained to do, his hands were busy at the fly of his little blue britches, from which a stream was issuing, splashing down on his white stockings and the buckles of his princely shoes. Perhaps that thunderbolt with which I had threatened the crying children, in a watered-down form so to speak, had struck me instead.

But as the years were to prove, time and again, neither thunderbolts, fire, flood, pestilence, nor human perversity could stop Universal's pilgrims of the impossible from raising their home talent curtains on 1,001 Broadways.

# "Stewart Wants Me for a Sunbeam"

*As the coaching graduates* of its 1928 classes fought and won Universal's battles on the road, significant changes were occurring in the company. First, it was rapidly growing larger. For a single training course in the summer of 1929, the Stewarts enrolled 102 girls, among them Billie Cook, Grace Barrington, and Margarete Morse. Such large classes proved unmanageable for the Stewarts alone, and they called on experienced coaches to assist them. Finally, the company was planning to introduce a new play, *Corporal Eagen,* while continuing to stage *Aunt Lucia.*

This play, which like *Aunt Lucia* figures in many coaches' reminiscences, was a three-act comedy of "American rookies in Army life" in World War I. It opened (again like *Aunt Lucia*) with a Baby Pageant which was now called "My Dream of a Big Parade." Instead of nightwear, the little girls wore white dresses and the little boys white shirts and pants. Also banked onstage were "soldiers, sailors, war nurses, and all the rest of folks that go to make up a war," as the *Fairfield Ledger* reported. Billie Cook recalls the lyrics of a then well-known song that served as an overture:

> Last night I was dreaming
> Of days that are gone
> Of days you might recall
> And just like a photoplay upon the wall
> Once more I saw it all—
> It was only a dream, you see
> But oh! how real it seemed to me!

> I saw buddies true
> Marching two by two,
> In my Dream of the Big Parade.
> I saw angels fair
> With the Red Cross there
> In my Dream of the Big Parade.
> I saw gold star mothers
> Sisters and brothers
> What a sacrifice they made!
> I saw one-legged pals
> Coming home to their gals
> In my Dream of the Big Parade.
> Millions of soldiers, millions of men
> All going over, I can see them again,
> Oceans of water, submarines too
> Millions of sailors, helping them through
> Millions of doughboys landing in Brest
> Marching and marching; but never a rest
> And then came November that Armistice Day
> When out of the trenches into the cafes
> Came Paddy and Abie and Jimmy and Jack
> And over their bottles of wine and cognac
> Telling their love tales of Jeanne and Georgette
> Those little French girls they had to forget.
> And then came the long journey over the foam
> But all who went over, didn't come home
> In my Dream of the Big Parade!

*Corporal Eagen* was set in the company street of Camp Shove-Off. The first characters introduced were members of the Awkward Squad, an improbable conglomeration of rookie soldiers, represented by eighteen or so prominent businessmen. Among the rookies were Private Plum, stuffed with pillows so that he was unable to tuck in his shirt properly; Private Pill, "born in Arkansas to be near his parents"; Mamma's Boy, who wore a big bow tie, red mittens, and ear muffs; Private Yumpin'-Yimminy Yohnson, who talked with a Swedish dialect; and Private Gloomy Mike Katz, who wore a gas mask because he had to sleep next to a prominent townsperson—with that person's real name being used.

An Irish doughboy, Red Eagen, was the hero. He told his girl friend Sally that he had been promoted to captain. Now she was to visit the camp, and he was in a dilemma. As an added problem he and his buddy Izzy had been put on K.P. and had to peel a large pile of potatoes that were dumped on stage. A song at this point set the mood:

> K-K-K-K.P., Dirty old K.P.
> You're the only army job that I abhor.
> When the m-m-moon shines over the guardhouse,
> We'll be mopping up the k-k-k-kitchen floor.

In the course of the show the potato pile served as focus for much slapstick, including the hiding of girl friend Sally, who had been mistaken for a spy loose in the camp. The spy had killed from 44 to 444 soldiers by injecting poison in some potatoes.

Red got his promotion at show's end, not to captain, but to corporal, through his improbable capture of the real spy. All ended happily with the Armistice being announced and a medley of World War I songs, which included "The Star Spangled Banner."

Specialty numbers scattered through the evening were a sailors chorus, a girls chorus, and a minstrel. The latter was called the Deacon Jones Minstrel and was done between acts, with both the endmen and the "high brown shufflin' gals" played, of course, by businessmen.

Could audiences or, for that matter coaches, warm to what seems such simple slapstick? Yes, according to the recollections of Margarete Morse. She writes: "The highlight of all my exhausting, hard-pressing, deadline, quick-action work as director of the military show *Corporal Eagen* was—THE AUDIENCE. My childish, nineteen-year-old mind was so keenly interested, I would almost forget my backstage duties to peek out or even run around to sit part-time with the audience. . . . When the show was played, despite rain, snow, sleet, hail, and below zero weather, and the audience laughed, clapped, cheered, whistled, and stomped feet, THAT WAS MY REWARD! My ego would state boldly to myself, 'GEE, I CAUSED ALL OF THIS. I created the whole thing here in this cow-town, blizzard-enveloped prairie, or mountain hamlet.' My joy, my inner thrill, was to hear that ring of laughter, the shrill whistles. . . .''

To launch this new play, the Stewarts needed more coaches; hence their summer 1929 class was the biggest to date. Half of this "motley crew" (as one participant described them) were to learn the new script, and the other half the tried-and-true *Aunt Lucia*.

Three on-the-road coaches were enlisted as teachers. A newspaper clipping names one as Gertrude Lamb of Sioux City, who appears in a photo of Fran's coaching friends. Another was Elma (or Alma) Lightner of Odessa, Mo. She was a colorful figure; one girl remembered she wore "rings on every finger up to the knuckles." She herself wrote that she entered each town as though she were being greeted by a brass band, saying to herself, "Podunk Center, you're my bacon, and I mean to send a big slice back to the Stewarts." She was to help teach other Stewart classes and possessed widely recognized ability. The third teacher was Franceswayne, well remembered by the girls in that class. Margarete Morse described her as "in harmony with everything, so kind to everyone.

She had a wonderful way of talking to people; made them feel great— and, of course, was busy every minute." Another wasn't impressed by Fran's looks or voice, which could be heard over any crowd as it belted out a song an octave lower than the others. Yet this trainee respected her as being "on the ball" and "knowing what it took to get the job done."

Earlier that year Fran had ended her first year with Universal by directing in Winchester, Tenn., and then worked six weeks for the Memphis *Press-Scimitar* before going home on vacation, where she received the Stewarts' teaching invitation. She was thrilled. It was a chance to get her hand on the throttle and to impress her bosses. Newspapering had been all right, but there was nothing like directing home talent. She knew this now more than ever.

The teaching followed the routines that Fran had learned as a student, except that she now had a different perspective on the trainees. To get on her good side students bought her gifts and took her to lunch. She learned that all girls in the class had some college experience and about half were ex-schoolteachers out for adventure. Quite a few had either been disappointed in love, were divorced, or had quarreled with their families, and so wanted to get away, be their own bosses, and make some quick, easy money.

Many students had participated in school dramatics and thought they had come to Universal for "drama with a broad a." But "the promotion angle is what really counts," Fran wrote later, "and the directing is the leisure part of the job. They did not seem to take seriously selling ads, interviewing prospective talent, writing publicity stories, and managing ticket sales. Consequently, since they worked on commission, they failed to make money. Out of eighty girls who graduated, only twenty were left on the road by the end of the next year."

The newly trained coaches posed for an impressive graduation picture with the "old girls," also numbering eighty, whom the Stewarts called back from the road for a convention. Then the newcomers were launched on their first assignments. The veteran staffers stayed for several days of Stewart-conducted lectures and round-table conferences. Private discussions also were held with each girl on her performance.

Plans for the coming year provided the convention's theme. Primary emphasis fell on highly polished promotion that combined the experiences of both headquarters and the proven road performers. The *Corporal Eagen* and *Aunt Lucia* directors were pitted against each other in contests to see which could make the highest profits. If *Corporal Eagen* wasn't as good a script, as some directors said, high-pressure publicity would make up for the difference. Who could resist, for example, wanting to see a play that Billie Cook and her colleagues advertised in a two-page spread surrounded by merchants' ads and cartoons, as "a merry mixture of music, minstrels and khaki komedy, chock-full of nonsense and horseplay. . . . You will be mad at yourself if you miss it."

For the experienced directors, returning for these planning sessions was like homecoming week, a sorority get-together, and commencement all mixed into one. These young women had had almost no time or opportunity for communication with each other since leaving Fairfield. Now in evening get-togethers they all tried to talk at once. No matter who told the first story, there were immediately ten or twenty others who could top it with adventures that were bigger, more harrowing, or more exciting. Gathered in groups of special friends, the girls talked until morning.

Fran felt that her little clique was the most devil-may-care of them all. It included her training-class pals Isabel Jane and Ethel Jeanne as well as some others. She dubbed them the "Dirty Dozen."

All were capable of making good money for the company. All affected the attitude, "Nuts to this job. I'm out having a good time. I've got my tongue in my cheek and a dollar in my purse and good-looking clothes in my trunk, and what more can you ask of life?" They took delight in razzing the business policies, strict rules, and all the tommyrot the brothers put out about do or die for Universal. But under all this they harbored a real regard for their bosses, their company, and their show business calling.

When the Stewarts decided to crown the two days with a banquet in honor of their coaches, the Dirty Dozen decided to wear evening dresses. They knew it would anger the less successful girls who hadn't been able to afford such splendor. Oh, well, all the more fun in doing it.

About noon of the festive day, Fran happened to overhear one of the Stewarts say that he wished they had some banquet entertainment in addition to the scheduled speeches. In a burst of inspiration she volunteered, "Okay, let me get up a chorus singing the praises of the company and train a few of the gals to sing it. You know. Something about do or die." The brothers agreed, although Wilson said he would have to approve the words before they were sung.

After she had roughed out a skit, Fran had some difficulty rounding up the Dirty Dozen from naps, beauty shops, and ice cream parlors. She barely had time to teach them the words and dance routine before getting dressed for the banquet.

Meanwhile things were not going well for the Stewarts. Several organizations canceled shows unexpectedly, and the brothers were worried about having enough towns to accommodate their girls. Worse still, a delegation of coaches, not including the Dirty Dozen, showed up in their office sporting a list of grievances. Mainly they complained of the rigid daily procedure, of being discouraged from using their own originality, of the constant written reports, and of being treated like "beasts of burden" instead of human beings. The brothers were furious. They had decided to splurge by giving their girls a banquet, and Fran felt they thought that here were these ranting, raving old maids criticizing them.

At the banquet Fran sensed their ugly mood right away. To be sure, the Stewarts tried to look at everyone in that noncommittal way they had, but to her they appeared "weary, worn, and wan." When Wilson asked Fran to show him the words of the song and she responded that she didn't have a copy with her, he snapped back, "Then forget it." Did he mean that? After all the work she had put into it?

"Look, kid," he explained, "there are a bunch of girls here who haven't got the right slant on the company spirit. If you got up and tried to sing about it, they'd swear we put you up to it, and the whole thing would end in a riot."

Raymond, who was to be toastmaster, didn't arrive until the last minute. He had time only to shake hands with the visiting dignitaries and nod to his brothers.

Naturally the Dirty Dozen were disappointed when Fran told them their act was canceled. But they made up for it by flaunting their finery as they ate their soup, chicken à la king, and gelatin salad.

As brick ice cream and Nabiscos were served, the speeches began. One surprise followed another. The local postmistress gave a fluttery little speech telling how the company sent and received so much mail that she had had to hire three extra helpers this year. The mayor praised the virtues of the four brothers who had built such a big organization and had made the name of Fairfield, Iowa, known from coast to coast. He thanked the Stewarts, he thanked the girls, and he thanked God for the occasion. The girls clapped furiously.

After that the company really outdid itself. Raymond presented ten-dollar gold pieces to the girls who had been there a year, five-dollar ones to those who had been there six months, and two and one-half dollars to those who had come in the spring. The unlooked-for generosity stunned nearly everyone. This was perhaps the logical place to end the banquet, but Raymond was on his feet again. Fran noticed that Wilson was trying unsuccessfully to signal him.

"Now we have a special treat coming," began the emcee. Wilson almost rose and then changed his mind. "There is one girl in our organization who has probably been bawled out, browbeaten, and razzed more than anyone else. She came up here a smart aleck kid, so every time she tried to say something, we felt it was our duty to take her down a peg."

There were a few guffaws from the Dirty Dozen and polite laughter elsewhere.

"So imagine my surprise today when she was the one who suggested that she write a little stunt or ditty, or what have you, just to show that she could still sing the praises of Universal. We've decided to let bygones by bygones and hear what she has to sing about. Of course you all know who I'm talking about—Allen!"

There was thunderous applause from the girls. Fran glanced nervously at Wils. He looked confused but nodded assent. So the giggling Dirty Dozen clustered behind the piano for their grand entrance. Fran felt wobbly. The stunt she had written had caused mirth in her crowd, although a few had wondered if it ridiculed the company too much." To that objection she had laughed and answered, "Oh, you're afraid for nothing. I really think the Stewarts have a sense of humor if you catch 'em just right."

"Just right." Well, this evening they weren't just right. It didn't make any sense to go ahead. She was a dimwit if she didn't call it off. Still the girls were behind the piano ready to go, and Tillie, the lanky girl from Nebraska who looked like a cat yawning when she grinned, was playing the introduction.

The Dirty Dozen entered burlesquing the chorus routine that every girl in the room hated, but had taught and retaught to high school girls. There were a few smothered laughs. This made Fran feel a bit easier.

Whoom! The pianist played a crashing chord, the girls made an exaggerated curtsy, and Tillie started another number. It had a syncopated swing and the Stewarts, sons of a Methodist minister, recognized it immediately. In a few seconds so did everyone else, and there were more smothered laughs. It was the old Sunday school hymn "Jesus Wants Me for a Sunbeam."

Fran led the line, while the others swayed like hula dancers. She sang the verse:

> I took myself out to Fairfield
> Way out in Iowaaaay
> Spent all my papa's money
> Learning how to coach a play;
> For there are four Stewarts in Iowa
> Out where the tall corn grows.
> They are making a million bucks yearly
> Because I stage their shows.

And the chorus sang:

> A sunbeam.   A sunbeam.
> Stewart wants you for a sunbeam.
> A sunbeam.   A sunbeam.
> Now who'd be a sunbeam for him?

Fran continued:

> They are looking for pilgrims
> Of the impossible it seems.

> What they really should search for
> Is syncopated sunbeams
> To shine for them each day.
> Then all towns would make a million
> Putting on this goofy play.

The chorus sang again, and then Fran sang:

> He writes the meanest letters
> That you have ever read.
> Time and again you're discouraged
> And you wish that you were dead.
> Then comes a new town to go to
> And you're pepped up and you know
> There's nothing in the world you'd rather do
> Than to stage this goofy show.

And the chorus continued:

> A sunbeam.    A sunbeam.
> Stewart wants you for a sunbeam.
> A sunbeam.    A sunbeam.
> We're glad to be sunbeams for him.
> BECAUSE

At this, the music suddenly changed to the Sophie Tucker hit "It Takes a Long, Tall, Brown-skinned Gal," to which they all intoned:

> It takes a fast walkin', talkin' gal
> To put a show across in any town.
> It takes a sticker-lickin', flapper-pickin' gal
> They can't turn down.
> Now she's not rough. And she's not proud.
> But she ropes in a great big crowd.
> It takes a smart baby. I don't mean maybe.
> To put a show across in any town.
> You heard me. I said in *any* town.

The last song had to be repeated twice, and the Dirty Dozen made a hurried exit to behind the piano. Never in her life had Fran suffered from stage fright and nausea, but she did now when all the girls were clapping, pounding with forks, and yelling, "More, more." She hadn't expected an encore. Dumbfounded, she and her friends slid into their places at the banquet table.

After the confusion had died away, Raymond rose. Would they all be fired immediately? Was there a smile on his lips? Yes, and Fran thanked her lucky stars.

"Well, we not only enjoyed getting 'told' by you girls," he said with a chuckle, "but it occurred to me while this stunt was in progress, that here was a group who had caught that indefinable something that spells success. You're right, what we want is sunbeams. Because, as you all get a kick out of knowing, not everyone can do your jobs. You are highly specialized in your line of work. As the song said, it takes a fast walkin', talkin' girl. That's true, and the closing lines impressed me also. "It takes a smart baby, I don't mean maybe, to put a show across in any town." Let me suggest that the next time you get in a tough spot, repeat that to yourself and see how much better it makes you feel. Finally, let me tell you right now, Stewart does want you for sunbeams! So I'll ask, who'll be a sunbeam for us?"

Everyone yelled and pounded on the tables.

Raymond continued, "Okay, with eighty sunbeams starting out of here tonight, I don't care if we have a bunch of poor bookings, a series of epidemics, or bad weather. I'll bet you can lick 'em. And I'll even go that one better. I'll give fifty dollars in gold to the director, pardon me, the sunbeam, that makes the most money on her shows between now and Christmas."

Someone yelled "Hurrah!" Others took it up. Someone yelled, "What's the matter with Universal?" The answer came back, "It's all right." "Who's all right?" "Universal!" shouted eighty voices. And the banquet ended with everyone feeling as if they had just attended a football game where their alma mater won the championship.

As Fran was leaving, Wils stopped her. "Write out the words to that song, will you? I want to have it printed on parchment paper and sent to every girl in the organization."

# ☙ 11 ❧

# On the Road in the Eventful Fall of '29

*"It's the biggest town* I've ever given to a beginner," Wils Stewart told Grace Barrington as he sent out this former schoolteacher in the fall of 1929. "But I know you can handle it." He gave her Casper, Wyo., and she didn't disappoint him. She cut $444.40—the best a new coach had ever done. She also made a success in other towns that fall, including Pueblo, Colo. and Keokuk, Iowa.

Large towns were plums, the best earning possibilities for a coach, but because of the larger problems involved they also could be disastrous. Sometimes in her despair and confusion, a girl would just give up and go home, and the Stewarts would have to find someone else to finish the job. Occasionally they had to stage the show themselves.

The Stewarts still were taking no chances with Fran Allen, despite her triumph in the sunbeam skit. They assigned her to Independence, Kans., later known at Universal as "the hardest town in southern Kansas." Fran was eager for that fifty-dollar gold prize for the season, and she could not help feeling disappointed in her sponsoring organization. It was a group of young working girls who met at the YWCA and called themselves the Owls Club. They obviously possessed neither affluence nor influence in the community.

One asset the Owls did have was their cause. They were staging *Aunt Lucia* to raise money for the Better Babies Milk Fund. That normally would open the doors to substantial newspaper publicity, so Fran hied herself to the paper. "Nothing doing," was the editor's response. He would give no free publicity, not even one story, to outside companies that came in to stage shows. Of course her money was good if she wanted to buy advertising. None of Fran's persuasion could set any milk flowing for babies here, and she left defeated.

She turned to getting her cast together. It was important to line up the big boys first. During the lunch hour, the Owls' only free time, some of the members took her over to meet the mayor. He was out to lunch. So was the chief of police. So were the others she hoped to sign up for her show.

Well then, she would start her round of the stores to sell ads for the handbills. She soon noticed window cards announcing the arrival in Independence of the most famous band in the country, the Sousa Band. It was to play the night before her own show and Sousa, always a sellout, was sure to attract large crowds. How many people would want to go out again the next evening to see *Aunt Lucia*?

Fran refused to be discouraged. If the Owls worked hard, they could still pull it off. She called another meeting, a pep session, and they agreed to push the tickets.

On her way back to her hotel that night, she noticed hundreds of cars parked around the Coliseum where a prize fight was in progress. To Fran those cars seemed providentially provided. She got out her stickers, which were small gummed labels with cartoon likenesses of Aunt Lucia. Across them in bold red letters ran the slogan "WANT TO LAUGH? SEE AUNT LUCIA." Fran cheerfully affixed one to every car parked in the area, by her count at least 300. So the paper wouldn't give her free publicity? At least all these people would know about the show. Glowing inside, she went to a restaurant, where she ordered a sandwich, read slowly through the paper, and made out a detailed list of things to do the next day.

When she started back to the hotel, it was late. As she glanced toward the Coliseum, she realized that the fight must be over because the cars were gone. A scrawny little man darted from across the street. "Where do you think you're going?" he demanded.

"A masher, eh?" she thought to herself. She held her head a trifle higher and quickened her pace. The man swung into step beside her.

After half a block he said, "What do you mean by putting stickers on all those automobiles?" A strange remark from a masher, Fran thought and continued walking. "You can't go around doing that," he persisted.

"Oh, I can't? Well, listen, brother, it would take somebody bigger than you to stop me," Fran replied coolly.

He grabbed her arm and spun her to face him. "I don't know about that. It happens to be my business to stop you."

She jerked away. "Hey, what do you think this is? Take your hands off me or I'll call a cop."

"There's no need of that, 'cause I am a cop. In fact, I'm the chief of police. See this?" He threw back his coat. His big badge shone like a Christmas tree ornament. "What's more, I've had twenty-seven complaints by phone and a dozen in person within the last forty minutes about them stickers you put on people's windshields. I'm taking you to the police station."

Fran started to protest that she had done nothing wrong, but he cut her off. "You put them stickers on the windshields, didn't you? Well, that's enough for me. You've got one on my car. You've got one on the mayor's. And you've even got one on the squad car. If you think it isn't anything to go around damaging public and private property, you'll soon find out different."

By this time interested taxi drivers, newsboys, and idlers had gathered from neighboring hamburger joints. She attempted nonchalance. She crooked her arm through the chief's, smiled, and said sweetly, "Is the mayor down there, too? I've been trying all day to meet both of you, and I'll be so happy to go with you to see him." Fran shrugged her shoulder at the crowd. She almost called to them to be sure to see *Aunt Lucia,* but thought better of it.

She had hoped that once the chief was away from the main street crowd, he would simply warn her not to do it again. But on the three-block walk to the station, he was far from communicative. Soon they climbed the station's wide granite steps to a room lit only by a green-shaded lamp above a desk.

Beneath the lamp a shiny bald head rested on a big chest. Suddenly the head came up with a jerk and the snores ended. Two socked feet swung down from the desk. A hulk of a man in shirtsleeves and suspenders spat a stream of tobacco juice that made the brass cuspidor ring.

"Here she is," said the chief nodding toward Fran. "Got her just as she was leavin' Bert's Restaurant."

"Switch on the overhead lights and bring her over," the big man yawned. Fran felt like a child who had been sent to the peach orchard to cut a switch for her own whipping.

The man laced pudgy fingers at the back of his skull, half closed his eyes, and said through lips pursed to enclose more tobacco juice, "Out damaging people's property after dark, are you?"

"No, sir. I just put out some stickers as part of my daily procedure."

"Your daily procedure, eh? Well, it's not day now. It's almost midnight. And you've kept me here answering this damn phone all this time."

"Honestly, I'm quite sorry. All I wanted to do was let people know about *Aunt Lucia.*"

"Aunt Lucia? Who the hell is she?"

"It's the biggest and best show that ever hit town, and I'm here to put it over."

"To put it over, eh?" His repetition of her words further exasperated her.

Fran suddenly realized that this must be the mayor. She seized the initiative as the Stewarts had taught her to do, and launched into one of those memorized speeches that was absolutely sure to get a big shot into the show. Both men looked startled and did not interrupt. But when Fran mentioned the Better Babies Milk Fund, the mayor broke in. "You doing this for the Milk Fund you say? No kiddin'?"

These men were politicians! It would be poison for them to oppose the Milk Fund. Now that would make beautiful publicity that the newspaper might print, if they *did* oppose it. But she knew they wouldn't. Now, mercilessly, she brandished her new weapon. Both opponents succumbed. By the time she left, she had promises from both to take featured parts in her show.

Despite her initial problems, Fran made a good cut in Independence. This success advanced her to fifth place in the coaches' contest, behind Grace Barrington and four others. Perhaps it opened the Stewarts' eyes too, for at last they displayed enough confidence to assign her one of their big towns. There it was in the telegram: GO IMMEDIATELY TO BURLINGTON, IOWA.

Burlington was a railroad center on the Mississippi River. Fran saw it as being populated by millionaires. Everything and everyone there appeared to her to be prospering. *Aunt Lucia,* too, had first-class sponsorship by the Woman's Bureau of the Chamber of Commerce. Everyone knew the chairwoman of the show committee, the wife of the owner of a large Burlington business.

Fran couldn't help thinking how differently the newspaper editor, the police chief, and the mayor in the last town would have treated her if she had been a social leader like this chairwoman—or a famous movie star or other personality. What would happen if, instead of entering this next town as just plain Franceswayne Allen, she were to enter it as a celebrity? The idea excited her. But could she carry it off? She could be an actress, perhaps. Not someone in the movies whose face was well known. Maybe someone on Broadway, or better still, on radio. Someone she resembled, someone whose voice she could imitate. She knew she was good at imitations, but could she sustain one for almost two weeks? She was determined to try.

It is not known whether she picked a real personality like Gracie Allen, as some surmise, or if she simply claimed to be a stage personality incognito. In any case the existence of her "identity" was made known under pledge of secrecy to certain leading committee members and townspeople. She pointedly told the papers always to use her "real" name in publicity for the show. Apparently she did a convincing job, for publicity proved to be no problem here. First, a story announced her arrival in town. A second article described her achievements as a home talent director and hinted at another more glamorous but unnamed career. One of the home talent stories declared that the Burlington show would be her forty-seventh production of *Aunt Lucia* (a real whopper of an exaggeration) and described the successes scored by this show. A newspaper photograph showed Fran directing the play and an interview cited her directing philosophy.

The townspeople were impressed. The chairwoman sent a chauffeur for her each morning to drive her around for ads and other duties. The merchants, thrilled to be dealing with such an important person not only advertised generously but also contributed prizes for two big show-night contests. According to detailed newspaper accounts, the contests would award the donated merchandise to various people in the *Aunt Lucia* audience: the tallest and shortest, the bald-headed ones who sat nearest the footlights, the oldest and youngest twins, the youngest and oldest redheads, the youngest post office employee, the person selling a ticket to the oldest city official, the largest family, the person who had come the longest distance, the most popular man in the Flapper Chorus (to be determined by applause). It was *the* game in town.

Fran also promised to do a number between acts herself, and the chairwoman arranged to have a maid backstage to help her change for it. Conveniently, Fran developed a case of strep throat and could not appear. She did, however, do an act for the Kiwanis Club a day or so later.

For an actress to play a role for several hours on stage is draining enough, but in Burlington Fran attempted to sustain a role for almost two weeks. Unlikely as it may seem, she successfully pulled it off. Best of all she cut $510 in Burlington, vaulting into first place in the coaches' contest.

Now all she wanted was to go somewhere and collapse for a few days. Little wonder that when the telegram saying, GO IMMEDIATELY TO CLINTON, IOWA, came she felt unenthusiastic. Sure, it was another large town, so obviously the bosses were pleased. But she was dead tired.

If the name Clinton sounded familiar to Fran, she didn't think too much about it until she looked at her map. It couldn't be true. The Stewarts couldn't do that to her. But they had. Directly across the

Mississippi River was Fulton, Ill., where she had done *Aunt Lucia* in January. She had gone all out there for the Woman's Relief Corps, which was raising money for a piano for the social room of the public library. She had used the *Clinton Herald* to the hilt in her publicity. Undoubtedly she had attracted many Clinton people to the show.

She considered canceling, but she needed the money. Much of her Burlington income had already slipped through her fingers. She decided she wouldn't use the Clinton paper except to run an ad and a brief mention of the show in the society column.

On the surface, her sponsoring group seemed a good one. It was the Clinton Women's Club. The club's drama department wanted to start a little theater and *Aunt Lucia* could be the first step. Unfortunately the ladies also planned a trip to Toronto immediately after the show's close. Everyone seemed in a perpetual flutter about this expedition. Little groups at rehearsals talked about the trip rather than concentrating on the play. That proved to be only the beginning of Fran's problems.

As in Independence she kept meeting setbacks. She learned that Universal's other play, *Corporal Eagen,* would be given at the same time in two communities across the river. Even more disconcerting was the news that the merchants already had taken generous ads for the film *Gold Diggers of Broadway,* a color talkie that would be showing at the Orpheum during her stay. The movie promoters had staged a contest somewhat like hers in Burlington, so that stunt could not be repeated.

Nor could she arrange a parade; the weather was inclement. Besides there had been a big parade at the end of September for the town festival. Another good crowd attracter, an afternoon matinee for the children, had been done by the Freiburg Passion Play only the week before.

The Freiburg production also made recruiting difficult. Nearly everyone in Clinton who liked to act had been a soldier, guard, or citizen then. When Fran approached prospects for her show, time after time she heard the excuse "not so soon." Only after extended effort did she and her committee manage to ferret out a cast and begin rehearsal.

Then came another blow. Fran learned that on the night before her show, a touring Broadway company with a cast of ninety-seven was scheduled for a one-night stand with *Rio Rita.* Its cast included Arthur Rogers, star of *My Maryland,* and Madeline Marlow, a famous beauty. It advertised its own corps de ballet, a native Mexican orchestra, and a chorus of striking, dark-haired girls. Almost as devastating, on the scheduled second night of Fran's show, the Ipana Troubadors would be appearing by popular demand at the coliseum. Fran's play would be shown in the much smaller high school auditorium.

She wondered if it was too late to cancel. Didn't the Stewarts know all these other things were scheduled? She sat down and wrote an angry letter, which she then stuck in her purse. The next morning she brushed her teeth, tore up the letter, cussed herself for a sissy, said her prayers, and went out to work with the Women's Club.

Afterward she wished she *had* canceled. Nothing fell right—except the snow. And how it fell! The day before the show it blanketed Clinton. That meant sluggish traffic in the spread-out river town for at least several days. It alone guaranteed a thin audience. But then came the truly serious catastrophe. For some time the stock market had been behaving erratically. By the week of Fran's Clinton show it was in real trouble. The play was set for October 23 and 24, 1929, and on October 19 stocks had dropped dramatically in rare, active Saturday trading. Monday there was a worse selling wave. This was the same day Fran's only ad appeared in the paper to announce ticket sales. It was terrible timing, but it could not be helped.

On the day *Aunt Lucia* opened, the market suffered another severe drop. That evening while her Tell-Me-a-Story Lady was starting her act, President Hoover was giving a speech on the emergency over NBC and CBS. Nor was the second day of her show any better. That day's market saw stock prices tumble in the biggest selling spree and wildest tumult in history.

Fran felt like an interloper as she worked with the cast. They were supposed to be having fun. They *had* to have fun to put on a good play. But how do you have fun when you and your neighbors might be plunging over the brink of financial disaster?

She did miserably in Clinton. Yet she was not the only coach to do poorly in that never-to-be-forgotten week. Evidently the Stewarts understood, for they gave her another town, Ottawa, Ill.; not as big as Clinton, but big enough.

In the *Bulletin,* Raymond sent an IMPORTANT MESSAGE TO EVERY COACH IN THE ORGANIZATION. It was highly supportive, as though he foresaw that the country was headed into a depression. He pointed out that they were now members of the largest organization of its kind in the country, for there were now 200 Universal coaches on the road. He told them that he and the company were "back of you." Fran felt a little happier when she read this.

She did much better in Ottawa on November 7 and 8, making a cut of $330.75 and shooting back into first place in the contest. She maintained her lead after her next town, Hannibal, Mo., on November 21 and 22, despite the cries of calamity and doom in the local paper. In the end, despite hard work in Kendallville, Ind., on December 12 and13, she failed to make quite enough to win the fifty dollars in gold for the 1929 fall season. Still that was no cause for a dive from her hotel window. On with the shows!

# $\approx$12$\approx$

# The Girl Who
# Wouldn't Stay Fired

*As the Christmas holidays* drew near, Fran was planning a different sort of show that might compensate her for missing the coaching prize. The Stewarts had invited her to be entertainment chairman for the coaches' convention banquet that would end 1929. As such she would help set the tone for Universal's 1930 season. Wasn't this honor enough for any coach?

Further and more important, if the Stewarts had liked that routine she whipped up in a couple of hours last summer, wait till they saw the extravaganza that now was shaping itself in her vivid imagination! She'd wow them, thrill them! Maybe they'd even invite her to come to headquarters to write their next play. How she was itching to do that!

As the convention gathered, she called her special friends together to work out the details. First, however, a more pressing concern arose for discussion.

Each dramatic director was scheduled for a private conference with the bosses, and each had been ordered to bring with her a complete set of costumes. The problem was that not one of them had a complete set. It is easy to imagine why. When a coach was on the road staging one show after another and promoting them at the same time, costumes were easily lost, overlooked, or pilfered. The coaches considered this normal attrition, but the Stewarts didn't. They ruled that the coaches must replace missing costumes at their own expense.

This might erode or erase the thirty-dollar deposit each coach had been required to make as surety for the costumes. Because that money would be returned when a coach left Universal, most counted on it as a nest egg. The costume requirement seemed a grossly unfair way to rob them of their involuntary savings.

Fran, ever willing to seize leadership, came to the rescue. Her solution was a simple deception that appeared foolproof, except that putting anything over on the Stewarts usually proved impossible. Most coaches could not seem to do a thing that the bosses did not know about. Grace Barrington, for example, was so poor in arithmetic that she could never add a column twice and get the same answer. Twice she got an accountant to do her checkup figures after a show, but each time a wire quickly came from the Stewarts: "Do your own accounting, Barrington."

Fran had been one of the few to get away with irregularities on the road. She had heard that Jewell T. Wilson, usually the winner in the coaches' high earnings contests, also flamboyantly broke the rules. At any rate, with Fran's encouragement the directors collaborated to make one complete set of costumes from those they had left. A beautiful set it was too, and just as it was supposed to look according to the rule book. As each conspirator went upstairs for her interview, she took this perfect set in her own duffle bag, suitcase, or trunk. She came out scot-free on costumes until such time as the Stewarts decided to make another costume check.

For the initial interviews all went well. But could it be that in that perfect set of costumes there was some tattletale detail that told the Stewarts something was up? A tiny cigarette burn in the same spot? A certain costume always ironed with an individualistic fold? Or did they simply know their girls so well that they were suspicious of such flawless costume maintenance? Whatever the reason, crime was suspected, and the ubiquitous Wilson was soon at the scene of the conspiracy, observing and nabbing the ringleader.

Now the conferences stopped. Now the remaining girls huddled at the foot of the stairs. Now the four brothers assembled in their office, their Peck's Bad Girl standing before them. At last Raymond spoke, his voice as even and unemotional as he could make it. "No girl," he intoned, "not even you, Allen, is bigger than the organization. As of now, you are fired."

Momentarily she was crestfallen. But this Franceswayne Allen was no longer the same neophyte who had trembled and wept before Marguerite the pianist only a year and a half ago. The rough-and-tumble of the road had amply tried and proven her self-confidence as a pilgrim of the impossible. Her prospects might be bleak, but now she saw being fired as no different from running into dead ends in Independence.

Her friends, too, rallied around. After all, she had done the costume bit to help them, hadn't she? Joy Kendricks had an idea. "Hey, look, why don't you take my first town after Christmas? I've got something else I want to do anyway."

One of Joy's and Fran's best pals from the training days, Ethel Jeanne Gardner, had now broken away from Universal. She had told the bunch that she was tired of having to turn over most of her hard-earned money to the Stewarts, so she had written her own home talent show and was starting her own company. It might well be that Joy wanted to see what the script was like and what Ethel Jeanne was up to. For whatever cause, Joy and Fran struck a deal.

Joy's show town was Lostant, Ill. Isabel Jane Fry was coaching a play nearby and agreed to help pull off the stunt. The sponsor was a Roman Catholic church, and the chairman of the committee was a priest. Everyone worked hard, and the show proved successful.

It is not known whether Joy wrote the daily reports ahead of time or Fran and Isabel Jane forged them. Again, however, something made Wilson Stewart suspicious. He decided to drive over without advance notice, slip into the back row after the director was sure to be backstage, and see the second night's production.

Almost immediately he could tell that the show wasn't Joy's style. The children moved with too much snap and assurance. The flapper costumes were too wild and imaginative. The final giveaway came with Aunt Lucia's grand entrance—a rough push onstage. Only one director did it quite that way. Even before Fran was called in front of the curtain at the end to take a bow, Wilson knew who the director was.

Now came the backstage checkup. Fran and her committee had started to count the proceeds. Isabel Jane stood nearby. Joy, of course, was nowhere around. Suddenly the door was flung open. An excited Wilson Stewart dashed in. "That's my money," he shouted. "I'll take Universal's share."

The priest stood up.

"This girl," W.T. explained pointing to Fran, "this girl doesn't work for me anymore." He glared warningly at Isabel too as if to say that she might be the next one fired.

"Wait a minute there," said the priest, covering the money with his robe. "Just who are you? I don't know you. I never met you. But I do know Miss Kendricks here." He indicated Fran. "She and only she will get any of this money."

Silence. Fran watched the expression on Wils's face change. What was he thinking? It always fascinated her to watch him in action. Yes, now came his ingratiating look. He had realized just in time that it was better not to pursue the matter. If Fran had rebooked the church for another Universal show next year, he mustn't offend the priest. "Very well," he said. Then, looking at the girls, he added casually, "I'll drive you both back to Fairfield when you're through. My car's outside," and he bounded out as quickly as he had crashed in.

The drive back to Fairfield was long and cold. Wils said little. He struck the girls as so like the warden taking two escaped convicts back to Sing Sing that they became almost hysterical in the back seat. After all, why should they worry—Depression or not? They were darned good coaches.

If the Stewarts didn't want them, they could go join Ethel Jeanne or another of Universal's competitors, such as Rogers, Ingram, or Sewell. Universal had booked some tough towns, and others were canceling because of the spreading Depression. If the company was to keep on its feet, it had to hold on to its best coaches. Finally Wilson told the girls in the back seat that he would give them another chance to prove themselves, but they had better behave and toe the Universal line. He decided to send them to different areas of the country.

What happened to Joy Kendricks? It wasn't long before her name appeared in the *Bulletin* on the list of those who had been fired. But for her this proved no problem. By spring, she and Ethel Jeanne and at least one other former Universal girl were producing Ethel Jeanne's play, and splitting all the profits among themselves.

Meanwhile Fran, the girl who wouldn't stay fired, and Universal went on to new adventures together.

# ❧ 13 ❧

# Getting His Teeth into the Act

*As Universal's* dramatic directors headed out on the road to put daily procedures into practice, they found that booze posed one of their biggest problems. Prohibition was still the law, but bootleg liquor flowed freely in many of America's grass roots towns.

Home talent shows offered hometowners a natural excuse to indulge. After all, the casts were signed up on the urgent promises of young lady coaches that they would have lots of fun together. Show nights brought the added impetus of stage fright. For many an amateur actor, facing an audience, perhaps for the first time, seemed possible only with an assist from a hip flask.

Grace Barrington recalls a little Arizona town near the Mexican border where, on opening night, her Flapper Chorus trooped onto the stage "drunk as hoot owls" and could do nothing but stand there blowing up and puncturing balloons. Another coach heard a commotion in the dressing rooms moments before her show was to start. She discovered that the Flapper Chorus had sneaked in some bootleg liquor and was sharing it with the high school girls in the adjoining areas. She locked the men in their room until their act went on. The best solution was introduced by Georgia Seabury who delivered a temperance speech to her casts. It worked well for her and was later adopted by others.

Franceswayne, herself no stranger to booze, was awakened to her most harassing experience on this score by an insistent knocking as morning light framed the windows of her hotel room in a little Illinois town. She had planned to sleep late, but the knocks became thunderous.

"Please, Miss Allen, it's me," lisped a voice. "It's important. I've got to come inside."

It was Jimmy, her leading man and a rising lawyer in town. He played the college boy who in turn impersonated the rich Aunt Lucia. Since the part drew two-thirds of the lines and laughs, Jimmy *was* the show.

Oh, no, Fran thought, he isn't drunk again! He had left dress rehearsal the night before in high spirits, after taking a bracer every time he missed a line. His parting words had been a boisterous promise he would be the best Aunt Lucia in the country. "Just a minute," Fran called as she slipped into her coolie coat and mules.

The actor who entered was no longer hilarious. His collar hung undone and his tie was pulled to one side. His hair was matted. Bloodshot eyes stared from an unshaven face. Spots on his vest marked a lack of care in tipping the bottle.

Sheepishly he slumped down on the edge of her costume trunk, holding his head in his hands. For a long minute neither spoke. Then, "I haven't seen a bed all night. It's awful," he stuttered, his words barely intelligible.

"We've got a show tonight," Fran responded briskly. "I told you when you left rehearsal to get some rest. What in the world's the matter with you? Have you lost your mind?"

Slowly and mournfully he shook his head. "No, it isn't my mind I've lost. I have lost. . . ." He gulped. It was almost too painful to admit. "I've lost my teeth." His lips parted, revealing a yawning cavity of toothless gums.

Impatiently she answered, "You're drunk."

He returned her stare with a woebegone mongrel expression that was both comic and tragic. "No, I'm not drunk. I'm dead sober. My teeth are gone. And I'll be ruined if anybody knows they were false."

He had lost his own teeth in World War I, and a dentist in France had fitted him so well that no one knew he wore dentures. Even his fiancée did not know. He broke down and sobbed, babbling incoherently that his girl wouldn't want to have a toothless husband.

What a mess! There were going to be two packed houses, but without the leading actor, there would be no play. It would be impossible to train anyone else on such short notice. Fran shook his shoulder and commanded fiercely, "Stop that sniveling. Tell me how you lost your teeth."

After rehearsal, he confessed, he and the local butcher, who was the butter-and-egg man in the show, had driven to a field some five miles east of town to sample a cache of liquor. It was hidden in a series of half-pints, carefully camouflaged behind every post with a hole in the top of it for two miles fronting a certain farm.

The first two half-pints had been easily located. From there on Jimmy became hazy about what happened. Distinctly, however, he remembered that while in search of a fourth bottle, he took a drink to the success of the big show. Unexpectedly he fell into a coughing fit and his companion had smacked him soundly between the shoulders. Out popped his teeth, disappearing in the darkness of the plowed field.

Not wanting the butcher to know his carefully guarded secret, he persuaded his friend to leave him in the open spaces to sober up. With the dawn he trudged back and forth along the bumpy terrain searching for his teeth. They were nowhere to be found, and without them he would not appear in the show. Described by his friends as the "toughest, fightingest guy" in the local American Legion post, he now looked utterly defeated.

"We've got to act at once," Fran said, with a decisiveness she hoped would buck him up. "I'll dress, and the first thing we'll do is go out to that farm and find your teeth." For an hour they combed the tall grasses around the fence posts. Then she saw from her watch that it was time to start attending to the many last-minute details back in town. Resignedly she took her place beside him in his roadster.

"Ohhhh," he moaned as the car headed toward town, "I feel so sorry for you. What are you gonna do?"

"You mean what are *you* going to do," she blazed. She was more determined than ever to put on this show, no matter what. "I didn't lose the teeth. You did. So you either find them or go to a dentist and get some new ones before the curtain goes up tonight."

"I can't do that. He'd tell everybody in town. Besides, it takes a long time to get false teeth made."

"Then borrow, beg, or steal a pair. I don't care what you do, but the show must go on." Her manner softened. "You can understand my position, can't you? In the first place, we can't disappoint the public. Furthermore, if I don't do this show, I'll lose my job. Look, Jimmy, you're the whole thing. All the other parts are extra. Regardless of what happens, you've got to be there on that stage performing tonight."

"I'll be damned if I will!" he shouted.

Fran's heart stood still. Supppose he meant that? Suppose he absolutely refused to show up? She couldn't do that part herself because the plot called for a man to impersonate a woman. An actress in the role would make real farce of this dramatic farce.

They pulled up in front of her hotel. For a moment she was paralyzed with fear. Then she said, "Now you listen to me. I like you. You've been a peach, and a good pal, and I'd like to be reasonable and spare you all the embarrassment I can. But I'm here in this town to do this show. Six hundred people have bought tickets. I can't . . . I won't . . . disappoint them.

You'll have to come down and stagger through that part some way. They'll probably never know the difference. A few might think you're lisping because you're tight. All right. Let them think that.''

For a moment she thought back to a show she had done once for a Universal competitor when she had everyone in the cast pretending he had lost his teeth. It was a very funny scene, but she decided against telling him about that.

''Nope. My girl would know better. I won't go on. That's all there is to it.''

She had saved her biggest artillery until last. ''All right then, pal. If you won't play the part without teeth, and if you can't get any others somehow, and if you don't show up. . . .'' She did her best Wilson Stewart stare. ''If you won't do that, I'm going to get up on that stage myself and tell the entire audience about your missing teeth. I'm not going to let you flop my show.''

''But Miss Allen . . . .'' Suddenly he was weak and helpless again.

''Ladies and gentlemen, I regret to inform you that there will be no show tonight. It seems that a certain prominent young lawyer whom you all know can't do the show. He has lost his false teeth. You didn't know he wore false teeth? Well, now you do.''

She slammed out of the car and ran up the hotel steps while he called after her, ''My God, listen to reason. I live in this town. This is the best hometown in the whole United States, and all my friends will be at the show. Say you won't do it.'' Then he shouted bravely, ''You wouldn't dare. You can't bluff me!''

She turned on the top step and shot a parting remark that she hoped would petrify him ''All right, if you think I don't have the nerve, try me! Just don't show up and see what happens.''

That evening the fire chief looked like a Red-hot Mamma. The judge playing Mae West had a ten-cent-store diamond on every finger and a Merry Widow hat perched rakishly over one eye. The mayor had dyed a pair of his wife's stockings green and wore them with the feet cut out. The doctor sported purple bloomers that hung two inches below the pink georgette dress his daughter had brought back from Paris two years before. Now he strutted back and forth as proudly as any Fifth Avenue mannequin. With curtain time near, everyone to a man was straining to out-flapper his buddies.

''Can we roll our stockings?''

''Do you think I should carry a powder puff?''

''I had to get out of my long underwear to get into this Sally Rand riggin', and my wife said for me not to take off my coat till just before I go on the stage.''

"Tie my sash, will you?"

Talk, talk, talk. Fran, applying their makeup, listened with ears that did not hear, for she was thinking only of Jimmy's last words, "You can't bluff me!"

When the last nose had been dusted with powder, the last moustache blotted out, and the last beauty spot painted on, she gave the group of brawny flappers a final reminder about kicking high and throwing kisses and hurried toward the room that harbored the town's deacons and elders. They were to deliver the barbershop harmony, "Sweet Adeline," as the college glee club in the play. She gave each one a bright beanie and a cane bearing a pennant with "Aunt Lucia" stamped on it in white.

"Everything all right, Miss Allen?" boomed the Methodist minister as he pulled the beanie over his gray hair.

"Almost ready," smiled Fran, not daring to wonder what would actually happen.

She looked into the room where the high school girls were giggling, shouting, and shoving as they donned their sailor outfits for their "Breezing Along with the Breeze" song and dance routine. "Remember, dears, always start on the right foot. Be sure and smile and sing, but no matter what happens, be sure you smile."

Then she hurried toward the classroom that the speaking cast was using for their dressing room. She sensed the tension and undercurrent of uncertainty, the intangible, inexplicable thrill of excitement always present on an opening night. To her alone something was different; "Aunt Lucia" had not shown up.

She attempted nonchalance while she deftly cut and frayed the crepe hair and shaped it into a goatee for the old professor in the play. She joked and talked about everything but the impending tragedy.

Abruptly the butcher bellowed, "Where is that coyote of an Aunt Lucia? Where is Jimmy? Has anybody seen him?"

"He was getting pretty tight at rehearsal last night."

"Rehearsal nothing," burst from the butcher. "I left him out in the country five miles from town this morning so dawg-gone loop-legged he couldn't walk straight. And talk! Say, fellows, that guy is the goofiest-talking person when his tongue gets thick. You should've heard him!"

Laughter followed this sally, and the butcher continued. "Oh, say, Miss Allen, reckon I better start out in search of your wayward wanderer? I know where I left him, and I can get him quicker than anybody if he's still out there."

"No, don't leave. I'd hate to lose two of you," smiled Fran, uncorking the spirit gum and smearing it on the chin of the man before her. Firmly she pressed the curly crepe-hair goatee in place and stepped back to view her subject. "Who's next?"

"But Miss Allen, I'm worried about Jimmy," insisted the butcher.

"I am, too," was on the tip of Fran's tongue. But she quickly substituted, "Don't worry about anything. It isn't good for you." Then she turned to the cast. "Everybody ready now? Okay, I'll flash the orchestra for the overture. Clear the wings while I get the children on the stage for the Baby Pageant."

"Everybody shut your eyes," she said to the children. The overture ended and the house lights went up, a signal for applause. She switched on the footlights and the overhead border lights, then yelled to the stage manager, "Take it away!" The big house curtain flew upward. The Tell-Me-a-Story Lady stepped to center stage and was circled with a chalk-white disk of light. The orchestra swung into the introduction, and the show was on. Come hell or whatever, it was on.

Fran always stood in the right wing during this number so that she could go through the motions with the children, smiling and coaxing them in whispers to get the right responses. Tonight it was all mechanical. They seemed like little flannel dolls in the land of make-believe. She did not feel she was a part of what she and they were doing as she had in other shows. As she went through the familiar motions, a voice inside of her kept saying, "Why didn't you hold the curtain? You could have held it for ten minutes, couldn't you, and given Jimmy that much more time?"

She argued back to herself, "He knows when this starts, and it's his business to be here. I have to get it over some time." She began to go over the speech she had prepared to give to the audience if he didn't appear: "Ladies and gentlemen, I regret to announce. . . ."

A voice bellowing at her elbow interrupted, "Miss Allen."

"Shhh. They'll hear you out front," she cautioned the butcher. "Whisper."

"I thought you'd like to know that Jimmy just came in the basement door."

She didn't hesitate. She hopped over stage braces and piled properties, and dashed into the classroom where the cast was waiting.

There he was, with his back to the door, putting on a black Aunt Lucia skirt. The oversized gray wig was already cocked on one ear. Slowly he turned and looked at her with pleading eyes and a sheepish smile. He parted his lips and disclosed the most peculiar set of teeth Fran had ever seen.

They were not his teeth. They were not any man's teeth, as far as she could tell. The row of white seemed so enormous that she was both fascinated and puzzled. It couldn't be possible that so many teeth could hide behind such thin lips.

"Well, how do you like your old Aunt Lucia," he questioned her in a high falsetto.

"Oh, pal, they're priceless! Even better than . . ." She looked around, remembering that she must preserve his secret. "You're a scream."

"I'm sorry I'm late," he whispered while she was putting on his makeup, "but I had such a darned hard time sneaking them out without anybody knowing, and then I had to boil 'em twenty minutes to sterilize 'em before I put 'em in my mouth."

"Where in the hell did you get them?"

It turned out that they belonged to Aunt Chloe, an aged and enormous cook who cared for his bachelor apartment. Every night before retiring she put her teeth in a glass of water on the drainboard in the kitchen. He had had to wait for her to do this tonight.

Two hours later, when the finale was over and Fran was sitting on the costume trunk watching the stagehands strike the set, she heard a couple of voices behind the backdrop.

"Best home talent ever staged here. Not a mistake. Beats some road shows they bring in here."

"And that Jimmy. He's a born actor. Boy, the way that Miss Allen made him up was swell. Could you believe that she could slip those fake teeth over his real ones?"

"He says he's going to wear them all day tomorrow to advertise tomorrow night's show. Why, everybody in town is talking about it. We may have to run three nights."

As the two Legionnaires emerged from behind the drop, they noticed Fran. "That makeup trick you pulled by giving Jimmy those fake teeth and all. How did you do it?"

"Oh, it wasn't hard," said Fran. "A mere trick of the trade, that's all."

"Tell us frankly, Miss Allen," the other one asked, "Don't you think that he's the best home talent actor you ever ran across?"

She smiled broadly. "Yes, he was great all right. I'll never forget this show. He outdid every amateur performer I've ever known for getting his teeth into the act."

# ⚛ 14 ⚛

# Men—or Show Biz

*Year in, year out,* good season or bad, one Stewart policy never wavered: dating and amateur show directing do not mix. Their coaches, they decreed, must choose between a Universal career and "playing around" with the local talent. The reasons were obvious. Late dating and drinking made for a poor performance by the exhausted coach, and wild partying damaged Universal's reputation with its often strait-laced customers and prospects.

The bosses kept informed through coaches' reports, local gossips, and occasional surprise visits to show towns. The Universal *Bulletin*s dinned their concern for good behavior into each coach's consciousness. In the fall of 1928 the *Bulletin* counseled, "Get older men in your show. Don't play around with the young fellows. You must sacrifice a few petty ideas of personal pleasure for the success of your work."

The Stewarts publicized the trouble experienced by conscientious coaches who followed wrongdoers in show towns. Letters solicited from Universal directors to drive home this point included:

"It makes it hard for the coach who follows that [the playing around] kind. I followed several, mostly from different companies, and it takes nearly two weeks to convince them that you aren't doing the same thing—Lucille Smith." "Because former coaches have dated married men and played around they think that is why I'm coaching. I had to have a rehearsal before I could get them working—Elsie Spencer."

The *Bulletin* published a letter from the landlady of a new Universal coach reporting that she had been going out with a married man from one to three-thirty every morning. On Sunday the girl had accompanied him to Chicago and returned the next day intoxicated. Again the Stewarts called for reactions from their directors. Isabel Jane Fry wrote: "I think she's a damn fool. And I think the married men in these small towns are damn fools." Franceswayne more charitably commented, "It takes a certain period for all girls to get road-broke and to adjust their sense of values, don't you think?"

Whatever else the Universal experience did for its dramatic directors, it obviously gave them a revealing course in relations with the other sex. In one Ohio town, all the sponsoring organization wanted was a playgirl, reports Pauline Fossler. When she assured them that she was there to work and was not going to be *their* playgirl, they wired Stewart for another director "on some trumped-up excuse. But Stewart was wise and told them they would work with me or cancel. The first night the chorus men were drunk and obnoxious, but I didn't scream at them. I just plodded along. The second night they were ashamed and cooperative. The sponsors made a nice profit, and the day I was to leave they took me to a jeweler's and asked me to pick out something I needed to show their appreciation." Georgia Seabury always wore a fake engagement ring for wolf protection and found it effective.

Despite all the Stewart fire and thunder against dating, few coaches took their strictures seriously. For Gladys Lindsay (Wood), "romance" was her "thing." "I never left a town where I directed a play," she writes, "that I didn't have another fraternity pin and a pledge of undying love. Some of those guys were great and I really did feel it was the real thing, but others were just a lark."

The bosses praised Grace Barrington in one of the *Bulletin*s, saying that she put on "good shows because she doesn't date," which was not entirely true. She went out occasionally and had two proposals while on the road. "It was common for men to follow a coach in whom they had developed a romantic interest from town to town," said Mary Crowley (Mulvey). Indeed, when a girl was coaching, "she could expect to have a boyfriend in every town."

And yes, the coaches' flouting of dating orders often resulted in wedding bells. Frederica Mintern (Reed) married an actor from the Beaus and Belles number in her show. Violet Benton McClure married Universal's most famous booker, L. K. Woods. Evelyn Thompson met an attractive suitor in her cast in Decatur, Ind. Later in another town to which he had followed her, he substituted for a cast member who had dropped out and Evelyn played for the pianist who had also quit. After that they put their act together for life.

A coach who wishes to be anonymous remembers tossing a coin with

Franceswayne when they had volunteered to coach two unassigned shows. The coin fell for this coach to proceed to Monmouth, Ill. There she met her husband-to-be. Universal lost most of its girls through marriage, Theda Fusch (Grant) was told by the Stewarts. Theda met her future husband while on tour.

"It is natural for directors on the road to have opportunities to go to dances, night clubs, and dinners," Fran Allen wrote. "Being used to many social engagements in college, I felt at first that I wasn't getting by very well unless I had someone in each town squiring me around. In those days I never thought particularly about whether the fellow had any intelligence. It was much more important that he was handsome, wore good-looking clothes, and, of course, had a car. These affairs were usually tame enough, both of us whispering sweet nothings and vowing that we were madly in love. Usually these dates netted a box of candy or flowers when I left town; then for a couple of weeks there would be letters, telegrams, special delivery letters on Sunday, a couple of long-distance calls each way, and perhaps a visit to me in the new town. By the time of the visit, I usually had a new heartthrob."

This attitude led to two bad experiences for her. One began with a cast problem. Fran had chosen a talented young girl for her chorus, but because her father was a brakeman and her mother an allegedly shady character, the other chorus girls refused to perform with her. Fran "had a devil of a time deciding what to do." Fortunately the leading lady ran off to get married three days before the production, so Fran starred the unwanted girl in that role, and she "stole the show." This "heroine who had come forward and saved the day" situation pleased everyone. Even the "snooty four-hundred types," who wouldn't accept her, did not mind as long as she was not in their chorus.

Meanwhile the committee chairman, who happened to be crippled, became infatuated with Fran. Sympathetic to his handicap, she did her best to be nice to him. This only made him more jealous over her going out with a younger cast member. Returning about two one morning, she found him waiting in the upstairs hall of her hotel. He "grabbed me, accused me of being untrue to him, and threatened to choke me if I made any noise. I really didn't have sense enough to be scared; I laughed in his face and told him he was screwy and that I was married already."

At this her would-be suitor's rage boiled over. He swore he would ruin her reputation by telling everyone that she was married and a worse slut than the mother of the girl she had let in the show. He called her names and "a lot of tommyrot." Finally Fran said, "Listen, you idiot, I'm the one who's going to create a scene, not you." She broke free and dashed downstairs. She told the night clerk that a drunk was running around her corridor and had tried to frighten her. The clerk got a gun and went up, and Fran "was not surprised to find the fool had vanished." She supplied a description that would fit any ordinary man and went to bed. The next day she had to visit the chairman on business for the show and found he had gone on a fishing trip.

If this incident did not slow Fran down, it was followed by one that brought her closer to the Stewarts' point of view. The encounter took place in a pleasant little southern county seat, population under 3000. Burgeoning trees, honeysuckle, and tiger lilies lined the brick sidewalks beyond which frame houses stood far from the street. Southern hospitality and gossip were rife. Here the United Daughters of the Confederacy was the sponsor and *Aunt Lucia* was the play.

City officials, from this town and neighboring villages, had been signed to take parts. Someone suggested that the mayor's son George would be perfect as one of the college boys. "He's just the type. He's home on vacation from Princeton College." Fran took due notice. The boy proved to be as nice as he sounded. He was not only tall but in a rugged way he was also decidedly handsome. He had acquired just enough eastern polish to make him very entertaining; he also owned a yellow sports roadster.

He agreed to be in the show. All the girls in the cast were much taken with him. They preened in front of him and tried to attract his attention. But after the first rehearsal, it was Franceswayne he asked to take home. She was elated.

The first night they went for a chocolate soda at the drugstore. The next eight nights often lasted until dawn and they had something stronger, for George carried the largest and most beautiful hip flask she had ever seen. She was never quite sure what was in it, but she suspected that it was "a mixture of juniper berries and canned heat."

Then came a wonderful Sunday afternoon. He took her up a mountain to a little old-fashioned inn for dinner. They were served fried chicken, hot biscuits, and chilled melon in a cool, quiet dining room by an old black man called Uncle Alex, who had known her date's family for forty years. They went to a shady, sandy-bottomed lake for a swim. Still later they sat in the roadster as they had each night before, emptied the flask, and looked at the moon.

Fran was to see moons in every state, "but no moon in song, story, or fancy was ever to compare to the southern June moon seen from that yellow roadster" while drinking from George's silver flask. She began to think, "Now here is a person I could really settle down with. He has money, looks, and position, and he lives in this grand country down here. This must surely be love."

Meanwhile rehearsals continued, and one hot, stuffy night's work with the cast changed Fran's ideas on her life-style drastically. It was two nights before the show. George didn't know his lines. Being in the throes of love's young dream, Fran hesitated to bawl him out as she would normally have done to a cast member. He had been led through a scene three times, and his lines were so simple that any grade-school child could have said them backwards. The cast began to get provoked, as their lines were stymied unless he fed them the cues. Fran had them all go over the scene a fourth time, but again he flubbed.

Her true coaching instincts began to emerge. Love is one thing, but the success of the show . . . well, nothing in this world could be paramount to that. Gesturing the cast aside, she strode across the room to George. "All right, pal, what's the matter with you?"

He looked dumbfounded. No answer. "Just because you're the mayor's son is no reason for you to think you're John Barrymore. You are holding up this whole cast, and there's no excuse. I won't have it."

Still no response. "Well?" she demanded sharply. "Why don't you know your lines like the others do? Are you stupid or something?"

Gradually the stunned look on his face turned into a sneer. "Why don't I know my lines?" he retorted. "That's what you want to know? Well, I'll tell you why. I haven't had time to learn them because I've been out until two o'clock every morning this week, that's why, necking you!"

Nothing could be heard but the dripping of a faucet in a nearby sink. The silence was more oppressive than the heat. "Showgirl! Showgirl!" the eyes around her seemed to be saying. "What else would you expect anyway from a showgirl?"

Somehow she had the presence of mind to snap out a flip reply, "Pleeze, Mr. Mayor's son. I'm only a poor working girl, and you wouldn't want the world to think you'd takèn advantage of me, would you?" She knew it was a feeble effort, but after a fashion it bridged the silence. Doggedly she went through the rest of the rehearsal, though she was stinging with shame and humiliation the rest of the evening.

She realized that she had lost face with the cast. The organization did not cancel, but if it had not been near show time and if many actors had not been related to the sponsoring club members, Fran felt sure the curtain would never have risen on that show. The cast went through their performance without much enthusiasm, and the newspaper did not even review it.

That night when Fran went back to her room, her head was aching. She looked at herself in the mirror. Who was this person staring at her? Wasn't it Franceswayne Allen of Columbia, Mo.? Of course. It wasn't a cheap showgirl who was just out for thrills. Couldn't all the folks see that? Couldn't they?

She spent a miserable night pounding her pillow and vowing to go back home where she had a family and background and could never again be put in the position of being a tramp. Then it occurred to her that she *had* acted like a tramp.

> I had given the chap every reason in the world to talk that way. He knew nothing of me except that I was a showgirl. "Showgirl." How I hated that name. I couldn't understand why just because I was in show business I should be treated like a common person.
>
> I kept saying to myself, just because I had a date with him, a few drinks, and we got sentimental is no reason he had to tell everybody. Why, any local girl would have done the same, and nothing would have been said or thought about it. From this line of argument, I finally deduced these things:
>
> A girl on the road, without family connections, cannot do the same things a local girl can because the men are scornful of her morals and the women jealous. Her actions will always be misconstrued.
>
> Secondly, I decided there are only three types of men in small towns who want to take strange girls out: first, the local shiek, good looking, well dressed, and possibly from a good family. Even if he merely takes you out for a soda, he'll manage to spread the impression he has had you under every fence post between there and the next town. Next comes the stage-struck goon. He writes stars for their autographs, but in reality has never been closer to the show world than the balcony seat at the senior class play. You arrive representing that intangible something he has sought all these years. He follows you around, calls at all hours, and makes himself thoroughly embarrassing. The third type is married and, of course, misunderstood. He is not necessarily bad, and, in fact, you are safer with him than with the others because you have something on him, and he is a little worried about being blackmailed. He offers to drive you around and be helpful. He will start out by saying, "I sure like fun, don't you? Now take my wife. (Here you want to say, 'You took her, you keep her. I don't want her.') Now she is one fine girl, but then she and I don't agree on fun." From that point you can expect progressively a grope of your knee, a glass of beer, and an invitation to spend the weekend in Peoria.
>
> For these reasons many directors are scared, disgusted, or bored by the men they meet.

After a sleepless night of such reflections, Fran's head was still throbbing in the morning. After dressing, she walked into a drugstore and asked for a bottle of aspirin. As she started to open it she realized that wasn't what she needed. If she was to live with herself, she had to keep on in show business. Yes, that was her real love. But how sincere, how really sincere, had she been about it? How good a show can a girl put on if she stays out half the night in a yellow roadster? Up to now, hadn't she been mediocre?

Mediocre! She remembered the contests the Stewarts had been staging all year. Not once had she been among the top money-makers. She had tried to tell herself that it didn't matter. But she knew that it did, and she knew what she was capable of.

She threw the bottle of unopened aspirin into her purse. She knew what she had to do. From now on she resolved to confine her dating mainly to crowds. She would be a good mixer, but she would be somewhat aloof, too. No longer would there be someone in each town to confide in. How far she carried these resolutions cannot be known, but to some degree they must have changed her life. In recounting them years afterwards, she wrote, "They have meant loneliness that I could scarely bear at times."

One pleasant experience with a man came Fran's way that spring, although it wasn't romantic. She had the happy faculty of liking older people and they reciprocated. Near the end of May 1929 when the sponsoring committee in Humboldt, Tenn., gathered to choose a cast, one member suggested, "Now if we can get old Pap Cresnap up there in skirts, it will be a sellout." He was a ninety-three-year-old Civil War veteran and beloved by everyone. Franceswayne asked him to be in the Flapper Chorus.

"Wal now," he mused, "I never have had much time for the women."

Fran persisted. "Tell me, who is your favorite woman character, for instance, in the movies?"

"I don't go to see them movin' pictures."

"Do you read the funny paper? Maybe you'd like to be Tillie the Toiler."

"Never heard of her."

"Then tell me some women you've heard of."

He thought for a moment. "How about Old Mother Goose?"

Fran breathed with relief. He would be in the show. "That'll be swell."

So they got him a dress and a basket, and he borrowed a duck, put a ribbon on it, walked out on the stage, and said, "That young show lady thinks I'm a slowpoke because I'm Old Mother Goose, but I got her fooled. I'm the hottest mamma in town." He wiggled his shoulder, rolled his eyes, and lifted his voluminous skirts to shake a leg at the audience, then hopped offstage.

He drew a standing ovation.

The second night was a very hot one. There was no air conditioning then, but he did his part. When he was backstage, after all the excitement and exertion, he fainted.

Fran had no water, but she always drank a Coca-Cola during the show, so she dashed this in his face. He opened his eyes and looked up at her and said, "I sure made 'em clap, didn't I?"

"You sure did, pal," she answered, "but I'm afraid this has been too much for you."

"Why, shucks," he said, starting to get up, "I'm good as new now. Just a little short of wind, that's all." There was a look of great joy on his face, for it was obvious that everyone in town had been expressing their longtime affection for him, and what more could anyone want? Fran shared this joy with him. Wasn't that what home talent shows were for?

"By the way, Missy," he added. "Do you know I'll be ninety-four come a week from next Tuesday?" But he never was. He died five days later.

# ≈ 15 ≈

# Flush or Dead Broke

*Like a Mississippi* steamboat gambler, Fran had a purse full of cash one week and was flat broke the next. Her experience was not unusual for of Universal coaches despite the fact that many made good money for the times. For example, when coach Martha Carson visited four former schoolmates who were working in Chicago, she found that in her first month for Universal she had earned more than the highest paid among them.

Universal calculated a coach's compensation as 35% of the company's cut and a small fixed fee. How this worked for top coaches is shown by contest records. Jewell T. Wilson, as winner of the 1930 spring contest, made an average cut of $253. This meant she earned $116.05 per show or $58.02 per week. In third place in the same contest, Franceswayne cut an average of $235.36, thus earning $109.87 per show or $54.93 weekly. This was good money in an era when many women's jobs paid $50 per month.

The middle rank of coaches drew considerably less. "We probably made an average of $75 per job," or $37.50 per week, Ada Lightner (Stoller) of Bellevue, Wash., recalls, adding that "not much was left after we paid our expenses."

Expenses on the road would be modest the Universal handbook said. "In checking with experienced Universal coaches . . . the average cost of board and room this past year has been from $8 to $10 a week." The coach, however, had to advance the money for travel, to be reimbursed later. She also had numerous small uncompensated expenses.

More distressing, the coaches occasionally had to grapple with show cancelations or failure of the company to book a full-time schedule. Further, one or more shows that turned out poorly could financially wipe out a coach who kept no savings, which included the majority. Many coaches were tempted to overspend on gifts for their families to show how well they were doing or on lavish dressing to support their professional roles. "I spent a lot of money on shoes and clothes," recalls ex-coach Mary Crowley. "It was a glamorous life." After all, this was one appeal of the job. And the coach's gambling instinct bet on making up for spending sprees by a big cut the next town around.

Some directors came to grief through this practice. One would-be coach, Florence Bergh of Mt. Pleasant, Iowa, reports she was not allowed by her parents to join Universal because "they had heard of the many times Universal girls were stranded on the road, had run out of money, and couldn't get to the next town."

The successful directors solved financial dilemmas by their own gumption. Just before summer vacation, Pauline Fossler, far from her home in Abilene, Kans., ran out of money when her last three shows laid eggs. The Stewarts paid the fare between shows but not home after a season. "How did you make the jump from New Jersey to Kansas, Fossler?" Wils Stewart asked when they next met. Her casual reply was, "A little waitressing will do it every time."

Fran Allen was among those often afflicted but never downed by a money shortage. She remembered that after a big cut in October 1928 in Chillicothe, Ill., she had taken several forbidden leisure days in Peoria, where she splurged on clothes. This brought her to her next assignment in Effingham three days late and with only six dollars left in her purse. She took a three-dollar hotel room, and it was Tuesday afternoon before she called on her committee. Then she was stunned to learn that the show had been postponed because the high school auditorium wasn't finished.

She also learned that a telegram awaited her, which advised: EFFINGHAM POSTPONED GO IMMEDIATELY TO STANN, ILL. Consulting her map, she could not find the town. It did not appear on her railroad timetable or bus schedule nor had the hotel people ever heard of it. There was nothing left to do but call the Stewarts.

She was not allowed to reverse charges, so the dollar-and-ninety-cent toll call came out of her pocket. After paying for the hotel and tips and something to eat, she would have less than a dollar left.

With fear and trembling over being so far behind schedule, she made the call. "Hello, Wils? This is Allen."

"What do you want?"

"I want to know what to do."

"Where are you, anyhow?"

"Well, I've had the flu," she lied, "and I've been in bed all weekend and so now I'm in Effingham. . . ."

"In Effingham on Tuesday?" He nearly blasted the receiver from her ear. "Good God, you were due out of there last Saturday."

She tried feigning a cough. "But I've been sick."

"Oh, yeah. You sound like it."

"Well, I have. And now I don't know what to do."

"As far as I'm concerned, you can go home. You're through. Go home and go to the hospital where you belong."

"But Wils, there's a wire here saying for me to go to Stann, Ill., and there is no such place."

"Stann? Stann who? Wait a minute till I look that up. . . . Oh. The town is St. Anne." He spelled it very slowly and meticulously as though he were addressing a moron. "Did you get that?"

"Yes, but I can't go there because I don't have any money."

"Oh, you don't? This is Tuesday, and Friday night you had ninety-five dollars. What the hell did you do with it?"

"That's my business."

"Oh, it is? Well, this is *my* business, and I'm only going to give you one more chance in it. If you want to work for me, you get up to St. Anne and wire me from there by noon tomorrow, or else I'll send another girl up there."

"But Wils, I haven't any money."

"That's too bad. I don't either. And I never will as long as I have a bunch of dumb clucks like you working for me." He banged down the receiver.

She dropped by the railroad station and asked the fare to St. Anne. It was seven dollars and eighty-five cents. "Thank you, just inquiring," she murmured. Back at the hotel she addressed labels for all of her baggage except the round hatbox and told the hotel clerk to send them to St. Anne, express collect.

It was after eight in the evening when she started on foot up the road to Kankakee, about 100 miles north, from which a branch line served St. Anne. A white cow near the fence mooed and nearly scared her out of her wits. A carload of drunks followed her and began heckling her. She turned aside at the gate of a farmhouse and yelled, "Get on down the road, wise guys. I live here, and I'll call my faaaa-ther."

A few miles later another car passed her, went down the road a quarter of a mile, turned, and drove by her slowly, then went a quarter of a mile the other way before it came back alongside. The driver asked her if she wanted a ride.

"How many of you are there?"

"What do you care?"

She told him that she wouldn't ride with more than one man.

He said, "Get in."

When she did, she saw a revolver on the front seat. He was the county sheriff. He scolded her for being on the highway unprotected at night. He had thought at first that she was a decoy for a highway mob. There had been a rash of car stickups. When cars stopped for a girl hitchhiker, a companion would suddenly appear from the adjacent cornfield, poke a gun into the driver's ribs, and take off with his cash and his car.

Fran was glad to get out of that neighborhood. Besides, even her hat-box had been getting heavy.

Arriving at the next town, the sheriff took her home, where his wife had just made doughnuts. The three feasted on these with cheese and coffee. The wife was furious to learn that Fran had to be in St. Anne by seven in the morning. Fran did not reveal she was out of money, but instead left the impression that she had missed her train connections. Against their better judgment, her newfound friends took her to a gas station outside town.

From the gas station she got a lift in an apple truck that took her about 10 miles, dropping her at a crossroad. Shortly afterwards it began "thundering, lightning, and raining to beat hell," in Fran's words. She huddled under a tree and smoked five cigarettes. Then the rain quit. Another car passed, went down the road about one-tenth of a mile and stopped. When Fran ran up, the driver asked if she wanted a ride and how far.

"Farther than you're going, I expect," she answered, "but any little lift will help. I'm on my way to Kankakee."

"Hop in. So are we."

At this point, she didn't care who was in the car or how many there were. They could be bootleggers for all she knew. She climbed into the back seat, put her soggy self under a couple of lap robes, and fell fast asleep. She woke as they were pulling up in front of the railroad station in Kankakee.

It was then close to two-thirty. At seven she caught the one local train to St. Anne, paying twenty-nine cents fare.

She was famished, but she had only fifty cents in her purse. She called the committee chairwoman, hoping to be invited to breakfast, but she was the county superintendent of schools and had already left home.

Now knowing the woman's position in the community and also that she would be out of town all day, Fran entered a nearby restaurant. She explained who she was and that the county school superintendent had suggested she make arrangements for her meals there. Then she ordered a steak.

While they cooked it, she made the program layout and before she left the restaurant, she had sold them a three-dollar space. After that she made her rounds and sold space to every merchant in town, taking in seventy dollars worth of ads by five that afternoon.

Elated now, she called the school superintendent, but was quickly squelched. "Oh," said the woman, "we aren't going to stage the show." Fran couldn't believe it. "I wrote your company and mailed the letter just yesterday." There had been a home talent show there six weeks before, and the sponsors had lost money. The Daughters of Veterans was not going to risk doing the same thing. They had voted to cancel. That was all there was to it.

Fran told of selling the advertisements, but that made no difference to the chairwoman. In desperation, Fran proposed, "Well, will you do this? Will you let me go ahead and use the name of your organization? I won't ask for any help, but when it is all over, I'll give you your share of the profit according to the contract, no matter what it is. And if there is any loss, the company will stand all of it. Now that's fair, isn't it?"

The woman didn't care to be bothered, but if Fran wanted to do that, she would have to put it in writing. So she did, without owning a single dollar in the world and with a bill at the restaurant.

The St. Anne newspaper was only a small weekly with a single issue before the show, but Fran made the most of it. She wrote an article publicizing the glories of *Aunt Lucia*. Although so far lacking a full cast, she listed the names of the few prominent people, including the high school principal, whom she had persuaded to take a part.

Where normally a two-column *Aunt Lucia* ad set forth the names of all show participants, Fran substituted glowing descriptions of various parts of the show. Under Flapper Chorus, she wrote, "Your leading businessmen will dress as women in this act and will impersonate such famous characters as Clara Bow, 'Peaches' Browning, Mae Murray, Tillie the Toiler, and others." The actors' names, she added, would be announced the following Saturday, and she urged people to read *Aunt Lucia* posters and flyers for the news.

Next she plastered the town with promotional bills. Soon the Daughters of Veterans became curious about the show and started to sit in on rehearsals. After a day or two they began to participate in the promotion. The show proved so successful that before Fran left town, they gave her a party. Since a local young man had been squiring her around,

the ladies got the idea they were engaged. The festivities featured throwing rice at the couple and presenting Fran with a bridal nightgown for "if
and when." "I nearly died," she wrote.

Other financial crises presented themselves to Fran in the form of
bookings that threatened to become no-earnings situations. In Mt. Vernon, Ind., for example, a production had been scheduled for the worst
time of year, just before Christmas. People were too preoccupied with the
holidays to take an interest in amateur dramatics. Many coaches would
have became discouraged and canceled, but Fran, broke again, had to
have the money.

Again she could look for publicity to promote the show only in a
weekly newspaper. Again she placed a powerful story. Instead of the
usual advertisement, she wrote a long one-column letter typeset to mimic
a letter to Santa Claus:

> Dear Folks:
> No, this isn't a letter to Santa Claus, this
> is a letter that is very important and should
> be read by everyone that wants to laugh.
> If you are a grouch don't waste your time
> for then you would have something more to
> growl about. But anyone that is looking for a
> laugh and a hearty one is naturally going to
> be interested in me.
> I am going to play at the Coliseum
> Wednesday and Thursday nights, Dec. 12
> and 13.
> I am the biggest and best event ever
> staged in Mt. Vernon. I USE 100 PEOPLE in
> the cast and guarantee you 1,000 laughs.
> That's a big profit in any ticket these days.

The letter, of course, was signed "Aunt Lucia."

Fran made a guest appearance before the Kiwanis Club, where she
directed its choir in a medley of the songs they were to sing in *Aunt Lucia*.
She also appeared as an entertainer at the fourth quarterly membership
meeting of the Chamber of Commerce. The attendance was swelled that
night with farmers as well as businesspeople who had come to hear a
distinguished speaker. The local paper reported that Fran gave a "splendid number," a "clever sketch of her own typing, impersonating the
broadcasting by Paul Revere of the news that the British were coming
during the Revolutionary War, interspersing it with all the attendant
noises and conflicting programs usually prevalent when a program of
unusual merit is being broadcasted over the air. She received a splendid
ovation at the close of the reading."

Despite all the promotion, she drew a poor house in Mt. Vernon, but by concentrating on selling advance tickets and ads she came away with adequate earnings.

Another type of money problem, perhaps her most worrisome of all, occurred over another holiday, Memorial Day. She had finished with her show in Tullahoma, Tenn., but she could not send the proceeds on to the Stewarts since the post office was closed. She put their money, around $135 in bills, in an envelope tucked inside her suitcase. Then she left for a house party in Memphis.

Due to a wreck on the track ahead, passengers on her train had to transfer to another, return to Nashville, and be routed to Memphis on another line. She reminded the porter to get all four of her bags, pointing out each one to him, but when she detrained at Nashville the bag containing the money was gone.

The loss ruined her whole weekend. Worried and scared, she returned through Nashville on her way to her next assignment and inquired at the railroad's lost and found office. They had no trace of the bag. There was nothing to do but write her bosses and confess.

They allowed her three weeks to recover the money. If it wasn't found by then, she would have to make it good.

She wrote to the lost and found several times while she staged her show, but without satisfaction. At its close she again retraced her steps to Nashville and demanded to personally inspect the lost and found. The custodian took her into a room stacked to the rafters with luggage, which he asserted was everything turned in that month.

She sighted her bag at once. Since it was not locked, he told her she would have to identify its contents before it could be released. She described the little picture of her father that she always carried, and he pulled it out. "I guess this belongs to you all right," he admitted. Fran's eager hands sought, found, and jerked open the envelope, showering dollar bills all over the room.

"Holy Toledo," exclaimed the man, "it's a good thing I didn't know that was in there. You would never have gotten the bag. I'd have been in Yellowstone Park by now."

"And if I hadn't gotten it," Fran replied, "I'd have been in jail."

# ≈ 16 ≋

# Fran "Fights Off" the Sheriff

*Not only* did Universal directors struggle to keep their own cuts but they occasionally also had to fight to save the bosses' proceeds. Franceswayne recalled that on the second night of her show in Jerome, Ariz., the committee refused to reimburse her for the advance tickets that had been sold. Meanwhile the audience was already filing into the hall. Fran told the sponsoring members that she would not pull the curtain until they handed over what they owed Universal. She went back to her hotel room.

Soon the two committeemen who had signed the contract were at her door. They had agreed to shoot craps to see which of them would pay. They rolled the dice on her hotel room bed. The loser presented her with 300 silver dollars, which she was sure would give her a hernia as she carried them to the hotel safe.

Another former coach recalls working with an enthusiastic American Legion committee. Everything was going so well that she got their consent to switch the show to a bigger auditorium. Several days later, the sponsors' enthusiasm inexplicably evaporated, and they began treating her with marked coolness. After the show they informed her that neither she nor Universal would receive any money because she had broken the contract by changing auditoriums without noting it on the contract.

She appealed to their honesty as American Legionnaires. She threatened that if they did withhold her money, every Legion post in the country would be informed of their default. After an hour or more of cajolery and threats, they finally relented and paid the company's cut. Only later did she learn the reason for their drastic change. One day she had slipped on a ring she owned because it complemented her outfit. It was a Masonic ring, and a strong anti-Masonic faction dominated this Legion post.

Fran made her biggest fight in silver dollar country to save a show's earnings. The bag of worms she walked into had its genesis in Phoenix, Ariz. Previously a coach, one of the few men Universal had hired, staged a show there and absconded with the proceeds. Like all coaches, he was bonded by Universal, so the money eventually would be refunded. Still the local citizens had no confidence that their money would be recovered, particularly from a home talent outfit far away in Iowa.

Shortly thereafter Fran was assigned to relatively nearby Prescott, Ariz., for a show April 24 and 25, 1930. A smallpox epidemic had broken out there, driving her "nearly crazy." Some of her actors were quarantined and, as it turned out, a complete cast could not be assembled until opening night. The last thing Fran needed on her mind was a problem from another town; but on the heels of her arrival, the chairman of the defrauded Phoenix group, a military officer, also arrived in Prescott. He informed Fran's committee that Universal had defaulted on its Phoenix show to the tune of $400 and would not make good.

The local committee was about to cancel, when Fran secured a wire from the Stewarts stating that the Phoenix case was under investigation and that settlement was absolutely guaranteed. This and further correspondence enabled her to patch things, or so she believed.

In her Flapper Chorus was Sheriff George Ruffner of Yavapai County, a pioneer from the days when the West was still rough and tough. Tradition had it that he was the first man to wrestle a calf to the ground in a rodeo. He was also well known for getting his man, whether it was an old- time cattle rustler or a modern-day trunk murderer, and he never carried a gun.

Now, "wrinkled as an old prune with a gravelly voice," he remained the epitome of a western lawman. Yet to Fran, whom he liked, he was "kind and sweet as cream."

For his chorus girl role in the show, he had prisoners at the jail paint a pair of his old shoes with red enamel. In addition, he bought tickets for everyone in the pokey so they could sit in the front row. They amply repaid him by howling, clapping, stomping, and snorting as he did his Clara Bow. Afterward he stepped across the footlights and said to them, "Okay, boys, that's all. Now while I get this garb off, I want you to head on back to the jail, and you know I mean it when I say by the time I get there, you'd better be back in your cells where you belong."

During rehearsals he and Fran became great friends. Before the first performance, however, he received a communication from Phoenix that put him in a quandary about what to do without violating his trust as a lawman.

"Miss Allen," he finally asked Fran, "how do you get paid?"

"I take my money out of the total that the show makes," she answered.

"You mean the only way you get your money for your work is out of what you take in on a show?"

"Why, sure."

"Well," he ventured, "suppose sometime a situation arose where you couldn't get the money. Then what would happen?"

Alerted now that something was up, Fran affected an innocent attitude. "I don't understand what you mean. I can't see how I could keep from getting paid, since I control all the money that belongs to the company until I have paid myself."

"Well, I'm not saying that it would happen very often, but being the law, I know of cases where I've been asked to take over the money because of debts a circus, carnival, or some hotshot promoter has left behind in another town."

Immediately she knew that he was talking about the Phoenix situation. "Oh, but that couldn't happen to me, because I'm not a circus or carnival or promoter. I have made money on these shows from the Midwest to here. Besides, God just wouldn't let that happen to me."

He grinned and patted her shoulder. "I hope you're right, 'cause I think you are a fine little lady and you work mighty hard. Anything you've got coming, I feel you ought to get."

"So he was practically telling me," Fran wrote, "that the officer from Phoenix had asked him to attach my show to cover the Phoenix debt, and that I ought to start making plans to get my hands on the money."

She began by asking the committee chairman to meet with her after the first night's show so they could pay all bills and make a first division of the profits then and there. In this way, she explained, they could save time the next night when they all wanted to get to a party the Jaycees were throwing for the cast at the Elks Club. He agreed.

Fran hid the resulting proceeds, about 100 silver dollars, in the pillowcase on her hotel bed after the room had been made up. She threw some dresses and coats helter-skelter across it so no one would notice the lumps. So far, so good, but the largest portion of the money would come in the second night.

When the final show started, Fran peeked from backstage into the house. There, with his military brass buttons and bars gleaming in the semidark, sat the Phoenix chairman. To her he was a sinister figure as he leaned back in his seat smiling and enjoying the show.

Just then Sheriff Ruffner came along. "Little lady, how are you tonight?"

She looked him square in the eyes and answered, "I'm fine. Why shouldn't I be?"

He chuckled and said, "Sure, sure. I just want you to know everything is going to be all right tonight, and I'm going to do my part to see it is."

She replied, "Oh, you were great last night, the hit of the show. I'm not worried about you doing your part."

"Just don't worry. I'm with you all the way," he winked and gave her a reassuring pat.

As the finale ended and the curtain fell, Fran buttonholed the committee chairman and sat him down on the stage to make the final settlement. Normally, she checked company costumes and equipment first, but tonight she said, "Don't worry about the costumes. I'll come over and pack in the morning. Let's get the money divided and get out of here. The easiest way is to say, 'A dollar for you and a dollar for me.' "

In Prescott in 1930, Fran had found nearly everyone carried silver and paid with it. So she and the committee chairman were dividing the returns in stacks of silver dollars when she heard the gravelly voice of the sheriff from somewhere below the stairs. "Now don't get fidgety," he was saying. "There is no need to cause that little lady any embarrassment. She's got a lot on her mind, collecting things and telling people goodbye. We'll just wait right down here by the door."

She began counting and stacking faster and faster, always aware that she must not arouse suspicions that might mean a recount and delay. The Jaycee with whom she was checking was maddeningly methodical. A haste-could-make-waste man, he slowly tallied the coins into his and her piles. When the count was over, it amounted to more than $200 apiece. The chairman offered to give her a receipt for the "cartwheels" and store them in his real estate office safe until they could be changed to bills in the morning. She was tempted, but feared he would give up the money if it was demanded by the sheriff.

"I told him I was bonded," Fran continued her narrative, "and not allowed to turn the money over to anyone else, but that if he signed the financial checkup sheet, he would be relieved of all responsibility." He signed, but then became concerned about how she would carry all those "cartwheels." He remembered there was a cigar box downstairs where tickets had been sold and went to get it. At last she was alone.

Fran couldn't wait. "Did you ever try to carry over 200 silver dollars? Let me tell you they weigh more than a Thanksgiving turkey," she recalled. "Also they have a habit of dropping, dribbling, rolling, and spilling all over the place. But I had an idea I was going to make a run for it if the Phoenix officer tried to stop me." She looked around the stage for a container and saw the duck sailor pants the chorus girls had worn. They were too bulky and the pockets were not deep enough. Ha! Aunt Lucia's gray wig! It was the work of a moment for her to dump her 200 dollars into it, jerk the shoestring from her sports oxford, and tie up the wig.

Even as she fastened the knot, she heard the voices and the footsteps of the sheriff, the officer from Phoenix, the janitor, and the committee chairman coming up the stairs to the third-floor auditorium. Sheriff Ruffner was talking loudly to give her plenty of warning. She was terrified. She had to find a hiding place quickly, but where?

A stage with the curtains and scenery hoisted out of the way is no hide-and-seek haven. It dawned on her that there was another well of stairs in the back of the building. She was not sure exactly where, but she set off in the probable direction at a near run. There were no lights in the halls, and twice she collided with pillars. Soon the darkness forced her to slow her pace and feel her way along a corridor wall. Her heart pounded so loudly that she involuntarily whispered to it, "Keep quiet. They'll hear you."

Voices resounded back and forth at the end of the corridor. They were coming closer. Aunt Lucia's wig seemed to grow heavier and bulkier; it would slow her down if she made a dash for it. What could she do with it? Hey, why not stash it in her ample bra? Scarcely slowing her advance along the wall she did so; it left her very top-heavy, but freed her hands. Now to find those back stairs. As she quickened her steps her heels clicked like rifle shots on the terrazzo floor. This would never do— off with her shoes! She leaned heavily against the wall as she bent to remove them.

"Whoom. The whole wall seemed to give way, and I tumbled into a lighted, procelain room," she wrote. "That was no wall I had leaned on, but a door. It was no small job to pick myself up overweighted with those coins, but as I realized where I was I almost shrieked for joy. It was the girls' rest room. My guardian angel was truly on duty, for accidently I had stumbled into the one place that could offer a woman sanctuary from an all-male posse."

Fran switched off the light. Sitting peacefully in a stall, she heard the voices and steps of the search party echo in the hall as they drew closer and closer and then receded. She heard the group descending the back stairs she had been looking for. Soon somewhere below, a door slammed.

Universal's cut was saved. Sheriff Ruffner had left lifelong proof with one admirer that a lawman's good deeds can extend even to *not* catching his quarry.

# ≋ 17 ≋

# New England Freeze

*Fran's worst attack* of loneliness and depression came in the winter of 1930–31. The increasingly hard times had not slowed the Stewarts. By the summer of 1930 they had so many coaches on the road, scattered over so much of the country, that they decided to hold several smaller conventions instead of a big one. Fran attended one in Columbus, Ohio, where she helped the Stewarts train a class of coaches.

That fall Fran took *Aunt Lucia* to Pennsylvania. Her sister Maxine had moved to Pittsburgh and Fran had asked for an opportunity to visit her. Fran did not realize, perhaps, that the Pennsylvania mining towns were among those hit hardest by the economic slump. If she had wanted to impress the Stewarts by making big cuts, this was no place to do it. She made double the effort, only to turn in unimpressive profits, and even then she was pulling off minor miracles.

If she couldn't raise money in these towns, at least she could raise spirits. People always had fun at her shows. In Easton she introduced a specialty number she called the Heinz Chorus, since Pennsylvania was the H. J. Heinz Company's home state. "She had all the old maids on her committee doing fifty-seven varieties of turkey trot," according to Isabel Jane Fry, "and the mayor, poor man, had to personally lick all the stickers."

In Old Forge, Pa., an inadvertent attraction was added. Everyone so enjoyed putting on the show for a church that they wanted to take a picture of Fran. The amateur photographer attempting this thought he could substitute gunpowder for flash powder. The resulting flame-up filled the auditorium with smoke. The audience almost panicked, but after learning the cause they enjoyed a hearty laugh over it.

The miners shared their meals with Fran. Even though in some homes the bread was spread with lard made of goat's fat and smelled of coal dust, she had never been offered warmer hospitality.

About that time, Raymond put Fran's name on a list in the *Bulletin* of those he'd like to have written contributions from. She failed to receive that issue, so in the next she was listed as a slacker. This so stirred Fran's ire that she answered him in page after page, which set forth her adventures in doggerel such as this:

> X is Xtra Xciting fireworks, don't you see
> When you start Xploding regulations in towns where you may be.

She ended with:

> You'd feel awfully funny sometime if I wrote
>     a real letter wouldn't you?
>         For as you know this
>             is just a little
>                 note, from one
>                     who is planning a
>                         lawsuit over the
>                             free use of "Slacker"
>                                 when applied to
>
>                     Allen

Despite the rugged going that fall, she often looked back on her Pennsylvania days as among her happiest. Her next assignment proved to be just the opposite and plunged her into depression.

Perhaps it was a mistake that she didn't go home for Christmas as she had always done, or at least visit her sister and family. Instead she went directly to Milford, Conn., where she was scheduled for a show early in January 1931. She recalled that on Christmas, when she got too cold sitting in an underheated hotel room and walking around the empty streets, she went into a waffle shop for warmth and food. There was only one other person there, a little old lady. Ever afterward that waffle shop in Milford symbolized loneliness for Fran.

The day after Christmas there was a storm with sleet and melting snow. At least now she could call her committee together. But trouble arose. When the members heard what a big affair the show would be, they balked. "Oh, no. we can't do all that. Not this time of year." The booker, it seems, had led them to believe there wouldn't be more than four rehearsals, that it was something like the *Womanless Wedding* with no speaking parts, and that participants needed only to dress up and pose picturesquely. They wanted to cancel.

"Wait a second," responded Franceswayne. "If the *Womanless Wedding* went over here at all, my show will be a panic."

"Well, maybe. But how are you going to get all those people to be in it? It can't be done."

"If it can't be done, it's the first time it's ever failed," answered Fran.

Reluctantly they agreed to let her go ahead and suggested names of cast members for her to contact. Then they turned to scheduling rehearsals. "Let's see," said the chairman, "we can't have the first one until next Thursday at the earliest."

"What's wrong with this afternoon?"

"Can't. It would be an imposition to ask people to give up their plans and come down on such short notice." The implication was plain: maybe where *she* came from things like that were done, but not in Milford. "And tomorrow's Saturday. That's out. Since this is a religious town, you certainly can't expect people to rehearse on Sunday. Nor on Monday, for that's when the Wheel Club rehearses for their minstrel." The Wheel and Cycle Club was the sponsor of the show. "Nor on Tuesday, for that's the big banquet. And of course Wednesday night is New Year's Eve."

"We'll see," said Franceswayne with the list of cast prospects grasped in her hand. With her committee aides, she called on these potential actors. First came the high school principal. He was delighted to be in the production. So was the head of the local factory; the president of the Business and Professional Women's Club; the chairman of the Republican committee; some teachers, including one who had been a Ziegfield Follies chorus beauty; the manager of a large nursery; a broker; and a host of others. Before anyone could object, Fran told them all to come to a brief rehearsal that afternoon.

And they came.

Now Fran was faced with something that had never happened to her before. Back in the mining towns, she had grown accustomed to working with simple, mostly unlettered folk. She had had to be patient, slow, democratic, and understanding every step of the way. Here there was an extraordinary contrast. The actors facing her were bedecked in fine clothes and furs in spite of the Depression, mostly well educated, traveled, polished, well groomed, and moneyed. They looked at her from under their arched eyebrows, she imagined, as if she were a servant or a menial.

Momentarily she felt vulnerable and perturbed. Just in time she remembered the advice of her old expression teacher Mrs. Harriet Jean

Trappe at Christian College, "If you ever get in front of a group and are seized with fright. . . ." How did that go? Yes. "Force your chin a little higher." There. "Take a deep long breath. Remain silent for just a moment before you proceed. Then instead of talking up to those people, look over their heads and talk down to them until you get your bearings."

So fortified, she launched into her introductory remarks. At once, a more typical Franceswayne attitude surfaced: "Damn it! Who are they, with all their high-hattedness? I'm proud of what I'm doing, and they aren't going to bluff me." She told them about her company; her morale rose as she listed Universal's accomplishments. She informed them that she was offering them an opportunity to work with something worthwhile. After that, she ordered them around just as she had the immigrant workers in some Pennsylvania towns.

The rehearsal was supposed to last an hour, but everyone stayed until ten while they went through the whole play. By the end of the evening, all were laughing and saying, "Really, this promises to be fun," and they arranged for a practice Saturday night and another one Sunday afternoon before tea, which they would serve at four-thirty there at the rehearsal. She made a sizable cut in Milford.

Immediately thereafter she lost a dear, familiar friend. In mid-January 1931 all the *Aunt Lucia* coaches were sent a new script and costumes and told to start doing *College Flapper* in the next town. For Fran this was Newport, R.I. She boasted in the *Bulletin*: "I did the greatest thing today I ever did in my life. I, Wayne Allen, went up and rang William K. Vanderbilt's front doorbell to ask him to be a flapper! Tie that."

She didn't actually see Vanderbilt. He was out of town as acting governor of Rhode Island. But she did sign up a member of his family, the honorable mayor of Newport, Mortimer Sullivan. He agreed to be the King of the Flappers. When the bunch did "Who's That Pretty Baby," the paper found the title "inadequate to the impersonations with their weirdly, worldly, and unwieldy attempts at rhythmic interpretations," and pronounced *College Flapper* the most successful show of its kind "to be produced locally."

She next visited Framingham, Mass., an industrial city near Boston, in bitter New England cold. The temperature dipped to –23°F and a powdery ten-inch snow blanketed the landscape. Fran never liked the cold. She also had trouble warming up to *College Flapper,* although she publicized it as having played all over the United States and Canada to "more than a million people."

Still more difficult for Fran to warm up to were aspects of what she now identified as the New England character—a certain restraint that resisted the kind of promotion that had become her stock in trade together with a contempt for home talent shows and home talent directors.

This attitude was especially evident in newspaper articles regarding not one but two rival productions in this Massachusetts town. No sooner had she started to select her cast when a dignified little story appeared on page one about a "community entertainment" to be given several days before hers and sponsored by the American Legion. It invited everyone, young and old, to try out for the show that would include only quality acts and benefit the city's unemployed.

The second competing production was *Peg O' My Heart*. The sponsoring club had brought in a college professor from Boston to direct it. The story announcing this show rasped on Fran's nerves as the epitome of intellectual snobbery, for it listed the many institutions where the professor had taught, along with a list of his famous pupils that read like a *Who's Who in America,* and told of his most recent production, William Butler Yeats's English version of *Oedipus Rex,* which had premiered in Boston's Symphony Hall. But what angered Fran most was a direct dig at her kind of directing. The professor, a news item said, saw "the wisdom of developing talent with an original, artistic expression. From the largest to the smallest part he discouraged any slavish aping of others," whereas Universal coaches used the copycat technique.

As best she could, Fran fought back. She placed story after story that stressed the local nature of *College Flapper*—the sponsoring Women's Club, the girls in the choruses, the babies in the pageant, and the flappers. A February 10, 1931, article reported, "Miss Allen said she felt quite fortunate in having a cast for the comedy made up of people who have had much previous experience." She was also quoted as saying that it took " a capable cast" to "handle" the action of her play.

She wanted it known, also, that her play was supporting a worthy cause, at least as worthy as that being touted by the American Legion. But what? An early report said the proceeds from *College Flapper* would go to the "Friendly Fund," which the club used "in answer to appeals for aid for worthy causes, most of them local." This sounded weak for that dark Depression winter in an industrial town. In a few days Fran was able to announce that the proceeds from her show, like those from the competition, would be earmarked for unemployed citizens. Next, in a publicity coup of cooperation, she arranged for one of her show's acts to be given at the Legion show, the Betty Co-ed number performed by high school girls.

By this time Fran was designating herself as "a professional coach from Dallas, Tex.," no doubt on grounds that this would sound more important to New England ears than Columbia, Mo. Now in full swing, she was snowing the professor with an avalanche of publicity. She placed a story in the paper almost every day, far outscoring him in volume. He did, however, strike back with one clever piece that Fran admired. It headlined the loss of a fortune by a local woman, extended sympathy to her and to the family as "one of the oldest and best known in town," and only at the end indicated that the incidents described were fictional and could be seen in *Peg O' My Heart.*

Fran's hard work resulted, as so often was the case, in a successful show with a respectable financial return. Then she headed for Hartford, Conn., not for an assignment, but to spend Washington's Birthday, a Sunday, relaxing.

The respite did not recoup her spirits. This Sunday reminded her of her lonely Christmas. She dashed off a plaintive letter that was later printed in the *Bulletin*: "I am a woman scorned. I glory in the fact that these New Englanders who go in for galoshes, dog and cat hospitals, tweed clothes, and boiled carrots, care enough to even scorn me. By the way, have any of you ever been scorned? I don't mean just moderately snubbed but actually scorned. . . . You coaches who would like to write a chapter in your memoirs on 'The Effect of Being Scorned,' just ask for a routing into this territory." She added, "I've reached the bottommost depths. We all have, and why do we stick? It's because we enjoy what we're doing and appreciate who we're working for."

As one reads the letter, one gets the impression that this was not simply a description of the situation in New England but a message to the Stewarts. She appreciated them. Why, oh why, didn't they appreciate, really appreciate, her too?

Her circuit through New England brought one interesting advantage, however. It gave her the opportunity to see firsthand some of the places connected with America's early history, which would be useful for her work the following summer.

*College Flapper* didn't wear nearly as well as *Aunt Lucia,* and she soon wished she had another better play to work with. Not *Corporal Eagen*, the play some of the other coaches were doing, but something new and fresh. Her imagination began to whir. She pondered over the kind of play she could write for the Stewarts. More and more, she sent them samples of her writing for the *Bulletin* or *The Universal News.*

What was the Stewarts' attitude toward Fran? By now their harsh earlier judgment had dissipated, but it remained slightly demeaning. They thought of her as an interesting eccentric they had learned to tolerate and were, indeed, somewhat fond of. At a convention once, when she was late, someone asked W.T. where Allen was, and he replied, "Who can tell? For all I know, she's over in Chicago walking a tightrope across the loop."

Despite all the hints Fran kept throwing, they still didn't think of her as their potential flush card, the one who could help them keep afloat and ahead as the Depression deepened.

# 18

# Search for What Might Have Been

*Fran's 1929 resolutions,* resulting from her bout with the mayor's son, may have put a damper on quickie, showtown romances for a while. Meanwhile, as her New England experiences brought home, the loss of these diversions intensified the built-in loneliness of the coach's job. As she wrote years later to her Uncle George:

"Never am I really any place long enough to make any friends, although I should judge my acquaintances . . . number conservatively 30,000, since I direct about 5,000 a year. Yet of all that aggregation I believe I can count my real friends easily on my ten fingers. I have visited in the homes of committee people, been thrown with crowds of my own age, but always, always, always, I have been LONESOME AS HELL. I couldn't tell anyone about this, because somehow these persons with whom I work feel that I have a marvelous life, that I AM somebody. Little do they know that more times than not I hit their town to live ten days on a five-dollar bill, which I dole out cautiously for 'coffee and' in order to afford a pair of hose or pay a cleaning bill to make me presentable at their big dinners or dances. At these I am always 'an interesting, entertaining, quaint, or diverting guest,' yet in my own mind I'm a fifth wheel, a nuisance, an oddity, and a misfit."

By the summer of 1931 her feeling of isolation had reached the breaking point. With her need for companionship crying for a solution, Fran surprised all her acquaintances. She made a spur-of-the-moment marriage.

In another letter to Uncle George she described the event as "meeting a man on one Thursday, marrying him the next Thursday, and finding he was a crook three weeks from that Thursday." She left Art (not his real name) for the good of "the family, friends, and personal dignity," only to discover she was to become a mother. Happy over this manifestation of God's will, she sought a reconciliation, but found the prospective father living with another woman.

"Rather than bother you with the lurid details," her letter continues, "let me briefly tell you that upon leaving him I was in an accident that caused me to lose the child and caused quite a serious back injury from which I have not fully recovered." She did not confide to Uncle George the worst aspect of the catastrophe. Only her sister knew that as she drove back from that unhappy meeting, her eyes fogged with tears, Fran had hit a gravelly shoulder, skidded into a farm family, and killed a youngster. This explains a collection of letters, all dating from that summer, testifying to her good character, for use with the police or in the courts if they were needed. They came from her minister, town bankers, and many other leading Columbia citizens.

Interestingly one of her testimonial letters came from Wilson T. Stewart, reflecting his possibly honest evaluation. He described her as "industrious, dependable. . . . She has ranked at the top of the organization. . . . She has a high moral character. . . . She has always been beloved by the people with whom she has worked."

The full impact of the failed marriage on Fran is revealed in an after-Christmas letter to her sister a year and a half later. She told how she had selected gifts for her sister's children. In a strange fantasy she wrote, "Art sent Ross [the eldest nephew] the football and drum—not really, of course, but he once said 'Do you suppose he could beat a drum?' And I said, 'Not at six months.' " The letter continued to recount a discussion of when Art might buy the child a football. "So," she concluded about the two gifts, "I wrapped them in his name."

She had not seen nor heard from Art since the accident but wrote, "I have never wanted to see anyone so terribly. I know it sounds maudlin, screwy, but you see all the Stewarts' wives planning surprises for them, and the boys making plans for their wives, and after you've palled around with everyone so you have a host of friends—but no one to really *care* or *share* with when it's holiday time—honest, I almost wanted to go out and rent somebody for the evening so I could make him happy and comfortable. I've got a perfectly swell husband, no matter what other folks think of him. Gee, if I could only have a Christmas Eve with him, and we could just pretend all the messy past of our lives hadn't happened, but that it was all great like in those grand first days. I play-pretend he's with me all the time. You are the only one I can ever confide this to, because you understand me so much and don't shame me about wanting to be my real self and not the wise-cracking, sophisticated personality I have to be with those I work with. Just sort of mention Art and me a little in your prayers sometime."

Other letters are equally sad. One to a relative recalled: "When I return to Columbia, I find myself realizing how out of things I am. Smug as my old crowd is, I never go through one of their precious modern kitchens that I don't have a desire to actually fondle the tabletop stove or the gleaming electric refrigerator. I almost babble incoherently at the vision of clever pottery, china, or linen." When at last she acquired her own apartment in Fairfield, she wrote that while her roommate, Mary Lee Wall (Zieke), hated to cook and wash dishes, "I love it. Honestly, you'd think I was Aunt Jennie remade to see me buzzing around the kitchen. I wash all the shelves and woodwork in the cabinets and stove, scrub the floor once a day on my hands and knees. I just love it."

She devoted pages in a letter to her parents to a shower she gave for Helen and Weston (Pete) Stewart as a newly married couple and for another pair of newlyweds. She described the elaborate place settings, the little poems she had written for each guest, the two miniature brides and grooms she had fabricated, corsages she had put together from thread and pipe cleaners, and many other attractive and amusing touches. The food was composed of two kinds of open-faced sandwiches, cake, coffee, pickles, olives, mints, and nuts. "I wished a hundred times you could have seen it."

No reader of the letter can doubt that these party furbishings and plannings mirrored her mother's entertainments in Columbia and that preparing them had infinite appeal to Fran.

But the happiness of a home and family were not to be for her except for several fleeting years. Fran would try and fail again and again to find a surrogate for her long-lost fiancé from Columbia. In the end the best she could hope for was to star on the home talent circuit. At least she could give that everything she had.

# ❧ 19 ❧

# New Plays
# Fight the Crash

*Universal coaches* on the road in the early 1930s got a grim look at how the Great Depression was shutting down America. In one Indiana town, Isabel Jane Fry reported via the *Bulletin,* "Every bank has failed," four prominent men committed suicide, and the local factory closed down putting 1500 of the town's 5000 people out of work.

Isabel's reaction was to "sympathize, tell the people they were doing a wonderful thing to have a show, and thus give people a chance to laugh and forget their troubles." For her lead she signed up a John B. Rogers Company director who was out of work, and he gave her much helpful advice.

In the face of the shattering economic climate, the Stewarts continued to operate unflappably. When President Roosevelt's "bank holiday" closed all the banks, Universal coaches and bookers from all over the country deluged Fairfield with frantic messages asking how they could continue without money. The Stewarts managed to pull funds together, and by postal and telegraphic money orders kept their far-flung organization functioning.

Home talent producers had one advantage for Depression survival, namely that their shows cost the sponsors nothing but instead promised badly needed income. However, selling advertising to merchants who were barely making ends meet and tickets to the unemployed or those likely to be, was like pulling teeth. Income from the shows fell into a worrisome decline, and many weaker companies went under.

Besides retaining strong promoters like coaches Fry and Allen,

**1 1 1**

Universal also recognized two other survival necessities: seeking new hit productions similar to *Aunt Lucia* and *Corporal Eagen* and beefing up costumes. Both would help Universal compete with Sewell, Rogers, and others. These companies were outselling Universal with some prospects by emphasizing superior stage finery and offering a choice of a half-dozen or more shows.

The Stewart brothers beat their brains and came up with *College Flapper* for the *Aunt Lucia* coaches; the new show was a reshuffling of the plot and character elements of *Aunt Lucia.* An improvement was also attempted in costuming. The Stewarts announced in a 1931 *Bulletin* that they would supply dresses for the women in the Collegiate Chorus, sixteen costumes for the girls in the Milkmaid Chorus, one for the King of the Flappers, one for the hero in his impersonation of the housemother, three wigs, eight sailor costumes, and six dresses for the Flapper Chorus. But *College Flapper* never achieved the popularity of its two predecessors.

In April 1931 the Stewarts copyrighted two new titles, *Fowl Play* and *Henry's Wedding. Fowl Play* involved shenanigans with chickens, but apparently never got beyond scripting. It was *Henry's Wedding* that became the money-maker of this second generation of Stewart plays. "The show is a steal from *Brewster's Millions,* I believe," wrote Fran. "I think it's a knockout." The plot detailed the frantic maneuvers of the hero, Jack, to inherit $10,000. To qualify he *must* be married by his birthday, and his old Uncle Henry must *not* be married. The action revolved around Jack's own marriage and attempts by himself and friends to prevent Uncle Henry's nuptials.

The play featured a number of black characters that would be thought racist today. Another crowd pleaser was a chorus that sang black spirituals. The production displayed a dazzling variety of costumes, at least for Universal. Several spectacular stage effects were calculated to bring down the house. As a final popular element, gangsters were introduced in the plot.

A training manual describes the action. The gangsters invaded the nephew's wedding festivities to steal the jewels from the wedding guests. They discovered Uncle Henry tied in a sheet, as the nephew's friends had secured him in an effort to delay his marriage. The gangsters kidnapped him for ransom. Escaping from detectives, the gangsters stashed Uncle Henry in an ash can. Shortly afterward, the black maid Eliza dumped gasoline into the can without noticing Henry and someone else tossed in a lighted cigarette. A flash of flame and a great burst of smoke filled the stage, and Uncle Henry emerged in blackface. Done correctly this startling transformation almost lifted the roof with a roar of laughter. Eliza, mistaking Henry for her husband, ordered him around until the real husband appeared, when she became hysterical. She called together the "Brethern" and "Sistern" of the Mystic Shrine to exorcise whatever demons were at work. They plunged the old uncle into a bath of holy water. Out of this he "came up white" in the second transformation of the play, which solved two mysteries: why Eliza saw two husbands and where the missing Uncle Henry had been.

Besides its lively action, *Henry's Wedding* introduced the greatest variety of costumes Universal had yet put on the road. "I carry eighty-five costumes," Fran wrote. "Forty of them are for the Beaux and Belles of the Naughty Nineties, which takes the place of the Flapper Chorus. The costumes are a scream—checked, plaid, and striped suits for the men and the usual Gay Nineties stuff for the women. Picture the characters— Daisy Bell and her Bicycle Beau, Broadway Butterfly and High-Stepping Johnnie, Miss Bustle and the Swain of 1890, Pantalet Girl and the Sheik of the '49ers, Floradora Beauty and Floradora Boy, Miss Hoopskirt and Beau Brummel of 1890, Lucille of the Merry Oldsmobile and Driver of the Horseless Carriage, Miss Bloomer and Henpecked Husband, Merry Widow and Celluloid Collar Benny, Anne the Bathing Girl and Joe the Lifeguard, Flapper of 1890 and Sheik of the Chicago World's Fair, Ball Player and Croquet Girl, Bloomer Bess and Gas House Harry, Miss Hobbleskirt and Peg Pants Charlie, Little Nell and the Cityslicker, Gertrude and her Pony Boy, Girl with Mutton Leg Sleeves, and Alexander the Minstrel Man."

Music for these numbers consisted of such popular old favorites as "Smile, Darn Ya, Smile," "Walking My Baby Back Home," "Yours and Mine," "River of Golden Dreams," and "The King's Horses and the King's Men." The latter was executed by the Maidens Chorus riding broomstick hobby-horses.

"The meeting of the 'Brethern' and 'Sistern' of the Mystic Shrine provides both a spiritualistic scene that is part of the play and also provides a chorus. You get the best men and women singers for this chorus, and they sing 'Lonesome Road,' 'Sing You Sinners,' 'Hear Dem Bells,' 'Golden Slippers,' and 'Hallelujah!' I think it is the best thing Universal has ever attempted," Fran concluded.

The company could be proud of the *Henry's Wedding* costuming. It had required a huge effort. If the costumes still did not fully compare with those of Sewell and some others, Universal needed to offer no apologies. Indeed, the Stewarts made a virtue of not competing all the way. In answer to criticisms that "the last company that stayed here had lots more costumes and scenery," the *Henry's Wedding* directors were taught to answer, "Well, I can see why you call this to our attention, and I do know that some companies have quite a lot of material, but here is the whole problem. We carry everything that is necessary for the successful production of the show. We have all the special costumes needed, and we don't carry a lot of unnecessary accessories just to make an impression. . . . We have cut down the cost of staging our production 100%, and consequently, we are able to make you great sums of money where other companies have failed."

The Stewarts' instinct about how far to go in regard to costuming and scenery at that time was apparently right, for they continued to prosper. Encouraged by the initial success of *Henry's Wedding,* they planned to launch into still another theatrical experiment.

# AN ALBUM
*of*
*Hometown Talent*
*on Stage*

*Princess of the Athens Hotel—little Fran Allen with Christmas gifts lavished on her by hotel residents as well as family when the Allens lived at the Athens.*

''Plunkety-plunk, daughters of a music man, if we keep this up, we'll be in the band'' *wrote Franceswayne under this snapshot. Little sister Maxine is at right.*

Mrs. Wayne B. Allen appears to be posting daughter Fran for a star-studded future.

Wow, what a hair-do! Fran tries out the latest rage as president of sophomore women at the University of Missouri not long before her fateful shoplifting dare.

Raymond Stewart, senior member of the Stewart brothers team that managed Universal Producing Company. Pictured as a champion high school debater.

Wilson Stewart, the "spark-plug" of Universal Producing Company, as a high school debater.

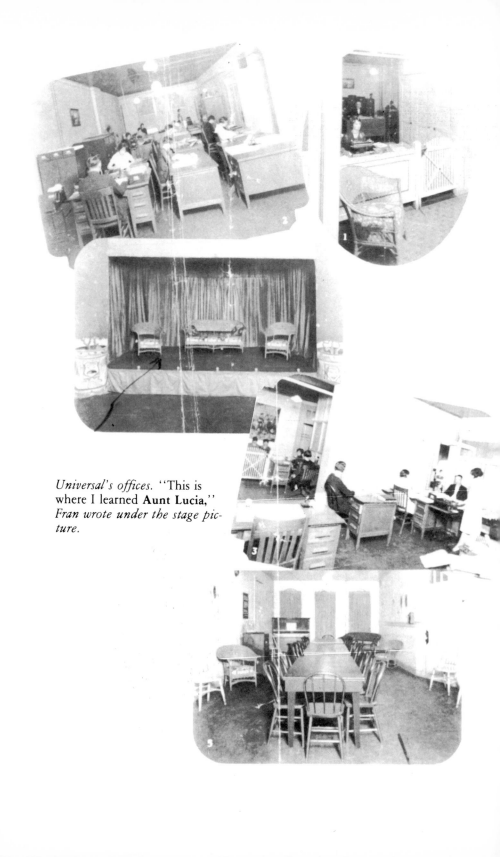

Universal's offices. "This is where I learned **Aunt Lucia**," Fran wrote under the stage picture.

*"The World's Largest and Most Successful Coaching Staff,"
proclaimed a* Universal News *headline over this gathering of
veteran and neophyte coaches. Photo was taken at the big
Universal Conference in August 1929 where Fran produced
her "Sunbeam" skit.*

*Before the end of 1930, Universal had made good its boast of
being "the world's greatest specialist in amateur productions"
by playing in all the towns represented by dots on this map.*

# THE UNIVERSAL NEWS

PUBLISHED BY UNIVERSAL PRODUCING COMPANY
Copyright, 1930, by Universal Producing Co.

VOL. 2          Fairfield, Iowa, October, 1930          NO.

# COACHES CONTEST A CLOSE RACE

## L. K. WOODS WINS BOOKERS CONTEST FOR SPRING, 1930

### Brozik Comes in Second And Fry A Close Third

L. K. Woods ran away with the Booker's contest for the spring of 1930 with 143 shows booked for the season. Woods set a fast pace from approximately the first of the year straight through to July first. In the first part of the season during January he was not up to the form that he hit in the latter part of the season when he really hit his full stride and started turning in from eight to ten and eleven contracts every week. Woods in his record for the season of January to June 1930 made the biggest record that has been made for a long time in Universal's booking history.

Brozik came in with 60 contracts booked for the season and took second place. Brozik started off with just a medium gait in the early part of the season in January but soon found his true self and started booking above quota consistently from that time on. Brozik did his work through the middlewest in Wisconsin, and Minnesota and through the northwest, namely in North and South Dakota and Montana. Brozik is in a class far beyond all looking for in that territory.

Fry, coming in close behind Brozik, turned in 61 contracts for the season and did most of his work in the west and southwest. Through New Mexico, Arizona, Colorado, Texas and Oklahoma, Fry maintained his quota and came into third place in the big Booker's contest.

#### Other Bookers Followed Close

Other bookers who followed close behind the leaders in the bookers contest were Thoreson who came in fourth place with Mallett in fifth and Dare in sixth place, while Carpenter followed in seventh and McQuaid in eighth place. Canfield came in in ninth place, and Morgan, Van Hon and Seaton came in in tenth, eleventh and twelfth places.

Other bookers who turned in exceptional work were Visher, Walton, and Stone.

#### The Booking Season Was Marked By Consistent Results

All the leaders in the booking organization in the spring of 1930 showed consistent results, and it was not any one particular week that put them over but regular consistent results week after week throughout the entire season. That is why Universal bookers are proving so successful everywhere today, because they are turning in consistent results and not spasmodic results.

#### The Booking Work Has Been All Over the Country

The booking work has been all over the country, it has not been in any one particular locality or one particular section of the United States, but all over the entire forty-eight states and Canada included. Bookers at the same time have been working on the Pacific Coast, Atlantic Coast, the Gulf of Mexico and in Canada. And continuously throughout the entire country Universal bookers have been carrying the message of big money, clean entertainment and community spirit to organizations everywhere.

#### Bookers Form "400 Club"

In the future bookers who maintain a quota of four shows each week are allowed to be members of the new "400 Club" and will be given pins similar to the coaches "200 Club" pins. The "400 Club" promises to be a very popular Club.

Winners of the Coaches Contest

January to June 1930

1ST. PRIZE
JEWELL T. WILSON

2ND. PRIZE
GRACE BARRINGTON

3RD. PRIZE
FRANCEWAYNE ALLEN

J. Wilson, the winner in the Spring Contest, was a "Corporal Eagen" coach and brought the banner of "Corporal Eagen" into the front ranks of the organization by passing "Aunt Lucia." The second and third places were taken by "Aunt Lucia" coaches, Barrington and Allen. Barrington taking second in the spring contest won first in the 1929 Fall Contest. The battle between "Aunt Lucia" and "Corporal Eagen" was a close one, from January to June, and "Corporal Eagen" won out. It is interesting to see who is going to be the winner in the fall contest of 1930, "Aunt Lucia" or "Corporal Eagen."

## J. Wilson Was First—Barring ton a Close Second With Allen Coming in Third

The big Coaches Contest from January to June, 1930 was the closest race that has ever been witnessed in the history of Universal's coaching organization. The winner was certain almost to the last, and only through consistent effort and hard work shows at the last of the season did J. Wilson come into first place, with a \$253.50 average. Barrington came in a close second with a \$253.18 average while Allen turned in a \$239.3 average.

Throughout the entire season the battle for first place in the coaches contest was a nip and tuck affair with about ten coaches contending constantly for leading positions. First one was ahead and then another, but on the final outcome, Wilson, Barrington, and Allen drew away from the crowd and finished in the first three places.

#### The Winners Came From All Part of the Country

Further proof of the success of Universal shows and the National distribution of same is proven by the fact that the shows staged by the winners in the first three places were in various parts of the country. Wilson did practically all of her work in New York and Pennsylvania, while Barrington did her work in Iowa Wisconsin and Illinois, and Allen did her work in Texas, Arizona, and New Mexico. This shows that Universal shows go over everywhere.

#### The Averages of the Coaches in the Next Seven Places Rank High

Close behind the first three places come the next seven making a total of the first ten places in the coaches standings, and all of them are high. Tye with a \$232.37 average came in fourth place, and we can state that Tye several times was leading in the contest, but fell behind on the final part of the season. Travers fighting every inch of the way came in in fifth place with a \$223.90 average and close behind her was only a few cents difference came Barton with a \$223.94 average.

Rankin from the far west in the California section came in with a \$220.96 average while Purcell, Ponder and Blackley came in with \$214.96 average, a \$205.29 average and \$203.52 average. In other words the first ten places in the coaches contest finished above the \$200 mark

#### The Second Ten Places in the Contest Showed Some Good Standings

The second ten places in the coaches contest showed some high rankings. This section was lead by Petrie in the southeastern part of the country and close behind came Fry Lawson, Rund, Aeschlimann, North Lockwood, M. Drake, Le Vitt and Fulk. These girls were staging shows in all parts of the country and doing it successfully.

A great deal of credit must be given each one of these coaches for the fight they made to maintain their place in the coaches contest Practically every one of these girls are back again this year fighting for another place in the big fall contest. And there is certainly going to be a great deal of interest around it.

#### A Great Deal of Outstanding Work Was Done By Coaches Ranking in the Second Twenty Places in the Organization

The coaches who ranked in the second twenty places were Dick, Fossler, Swift, McHugh, Heringa, A Drake, H. Baker, Martin, and Cook along with them were C. Andrews Rohwedder, Woodley, Warren, Lindly, M. Smith, H. Haas, L. Smith Adams, Craft and Chapman. These people held up the banner of Universal's coaching organization. They ranked in the order named.

---

*A coaches' contest, with Fran in third place, is headlined in The Universal News.*

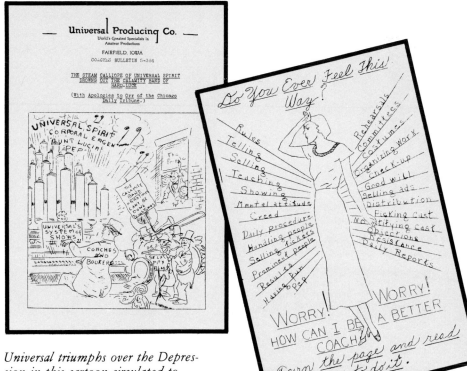

*Universal triumphs over the Depression in this cartoon circulated to coaches. Its calliope of Universal Spirit is shown drowning out the Calamity Band.*

*A pep-talk bulletin tries to buck up the coaches to meet Depression problems.*

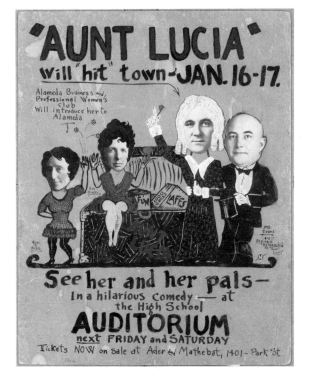

*Locally created poster added "'wham'" to an Aunt Lucia promotion in Alameda, Calif.*

*Wilson Stewart as Aunt Lucia, according to an accompanying note from Fran. The related article in* The Universal News *reviews the show's far-flung success.*

luction
llion
s

omedy
above
many

" has
has it
s and
n the
ds of
as low
gh as
n with
mark-

ucia."
ountry
se of

Th
has
Lucia
talen
is a
and b
ever
come
ducti
be a
tiona
Ne

Th
same
ship,
Prod
that
how
keyn
beau
and
th

*This handbill hails* Aunt Lucia *as the biggest event ever staged in Dodge City, Kans., citing a cast of 300 and 50 free prizes.*

LAUGH and **BE HAPPY**

"**AUNT LUCIA**"

The Great Collegiate Comedy

The Biggest Event Ever Staged in **DODGE CITY**

Sponsored by American Legion — Directed by Universal Producing Company

**300** LOCAL PEOPLE as CHARACTERS **300**
DON'T MISS IT! 50 FREE PRIZES GIVEN TO AUDIENCE

All-Star Cast Headed by Louis F. Miller as Aunt Lucia

### THE CAST

Jerry (the fake aunt) ............ Louis Miller
Evelyn (Jerry's girl) ............ Margaret States
George (college student) ............ Wesley Prosser
Betty (George's girl) ............ Betty Lyon
Dick (another college boy) ............ Carl Newby
Molly (Dick's girl) ............ Blanche Lopp
Collins (Dick's father) ............ Harry Grolier
Butter and Egg Man ............ Lou Meyers
Dean of Women ............ Mrs. Jack Saunders
Prof. Gaddis ............ Tom Phillips
Mr. Seemore ............ Ed Miller
Mrs. Seemore ............ Mrs. Ivan Swaim
Thorte, First Freshman ............ Ed Gill
Speed, Second Freshman ............ Paul Fisher
Fraternity President ............ "Shirts" Walker
College Sheik ............ Judge Karl Miller
Yell Leader ............ "Willty" Welch

### Glee Club

Judge Dunbar, Judge Miller, Ben Zimmerman, Carl Ray, Sam Gish, Dale Reynolds, Bill Warshaw, Ralph Newly, Ole Edwards, Hoppy Hathaway, J. Baugh, Vaughn Kimball, Ferd Dunlor, O. R. Cardwell, Dr. Certain, Jim Collier, Lane Dutton, N. C. Martin, Jack Faulkner, Charlie Russell, Jack Vaughan Ralph Matthew, A. B. Callaway, Donald Crimmer, Charlie Selig, D. Simpson, Luther Thomas, Ray Dadmann, Walt Bullock, Dale Miller, Bill Hulsey, Bill Weigh, Dr. Gribble.

### College Flappers

Tillie the Toiler ............ Harry Hart
Clara Bow ............ L. L. Taylor
Campus Flirt ............ Hi Burr
Girita Swanson ............ Dr. C. L. Hooper
Girl with the Million $ Legs ............ A. R. Zimmer
Flamin' Mayme ............ John Foley
Baby Face ............ Clarence Aten
Siamese Twins ............ Roy Buckingham and Cy Spreicher
Miss America ............ Clyde Smith
Mrs. Vanderbilt ............ Hal Minton
Dolly Dimples ............ Victor Kletz
Ziegfeld's Choice ............ Claude Gould
Vamp of Dodge City ............ Nelson Crawford
Queen of Sheba ............ Mort Williams
Peaches Browning ............ Harry Holmes
Shrinking Violet ............ C. L. Clinton
Irene Castle ............ Carl Etrick

St. Louis Woman ............ Joe Hulpieu
Vamping Venus ............ T. B. West
Broadway Chicken ............ Carl Fay
Little Orphan Annie ............ George B. Thompson
Little Nell ............ Gus Hardendorff
Ritzi Mitzi ............ John Pressley
Perfect 36 ............ Leslie Baldeston
Hula Lou ............ Si Perkins
Athletic Girl ............ Tom Reed
Dancing Girl ............ E. W. Nickels
Spinster School Teacher ............ W. W. Dwyer
Greta Garbo ............ Horace Pettijohn
Gold Digger ............ P. Q. Hanlen
Clinging Vine ............ Harold Skages
Chicago Lil ............ J. P. McCollom
Juan Crawford ............ A. C. Scates and Andy Byerne
Flower Girls ............ Chick Colison
June Bride

### Girls' Chorus

Gussie Allen, Margaret Manary, Theodosia Austin, Lillian Martin, Marie Brown, Roberta Summers, Norma Krey, Carrol Kennedy, Josphine Lutz, Margaret Small, Winifred Snook, Betty Kimmel, Betty Baker, Joy Whitney, Beth Anderson, Neva Striff, Mauel Winfrey, Marcia Long, Gwen Ginder, Eleanor Reighard, Evelyn Walker, Virginia Walker, Doris Crawford, Madelyn Hendricks, Anita Pires, Jane Ashner, Joyce Jeanette Diers, Maxine Edwards, Blanche Young.
Pianist ............ Miss Dorothy A. Warner

### Special Baby Pageant

"TAKE ME BACK TO BABYLAND"
Featuring 200 local children, ages 5 to 9.

### Musical Numbers and Specialties

Old Time Favorites (Medley)—Glee Club and Girls
Out in the New Mown Hay ............ Girls' Chorus
Specialty song and dance trio ............ Noisy Cannons
Who's That Pretty Baby? ............ Flapper Chorus
Breezin' Along ............ Girls' Chorus
Honey Gals ............ Girls' Chorus
You and the Man in the Moon ............ Entire Ensemble
Finale
Music by Black Hill Stompers Orchestra from "Jim's Place"

**DODGE THEATRE**
Thursday and Friday

**February 20-21**

Reserved Seat Sale at Dodge Theatre Box Office 8 a.m., Wednesday, Feb. 19. All tickets 75c.
Reserved Free. Special Matinee, for children only, 4:15 p.m., Thursday, Feb. 20. Admission 25c

*A Flapper Chorus to end all Flapper Choruses at Ada, Minn. Aunt Lucia wears the flowered black hat. Thelma Bump Duesenberg was coach.*

*Flapper Chorus for Aunt Lucia at St. Paris, Ohio. Here coach Pauline Fossler reported that the number of tickets sold and those in the cast just about equaled the town's population of 1,100.*

# SAPPROVE GAS FRANCH

EWS
RESS
ORS

Part of
Tasks,
Busi-

NS
APERS

Aanage
Home
Com-

eps its
Long
mill, a
and a
e com-

C. P.
s her
s that
ve at-

ll part
She
home
hus-
ore at
inter-
and
him
has
vhich
end-

K

## GAY COSTUMES FOR AUNT LUCIA SHOW

BUSIN
AWAI
OF C
ON M

Commit
Effor
Any
Dohe

SAY M
TO

McGre
ste
Sug
gai

WH
gas
the
field
"not
depe
gene
attit
bers
the
cide
vigo

T
of
tio
da
tes
frs

*Local actors, their heads superimposed on chorus girl bodies, strut in this* Aunt Lucia *publicity photo, a technique introduced by Fran. Photo topped a double-column article on the front page of the Springfield, Mo.,* News and Leader.

*Characters from an* Aunt Lucia *production pose at Buffalo Center, Iowa.*

*Handbill for Henry's Wedding in Shenandoah, Iowa, listing the local cast. The reverse carries supporting, half-inch ads of 58 local businesses.*

# "The American Pioneer"

## The Biggest Outdoor Show and "4th" Celebration Ever Held in Dallas County

## 600 - People of Dallas County as Characters - 600

The
World's Greatest
Outdoor Show

Spectacular
Thrilling
Patriotic
Sensational

# FAIR GROUNDS - PERRY, IA.

| SHAM BATTLES | **Saturday and Sunday** | 1000 BEAUTIFUL AND ELABORATE COSTUMES |
| --- | --- | --- |
| INDIAN ATTACKS | | |
| SPECIAL LIGHTING EFFECTS | **JULY 4th-5th** | PRODUCED ON THE WORLD'S LARGEST STAGE |

## BIG STREET PARADE AT NOON, SAT., JULY 4th

SPONSORED BY THE AMERICAN LEGION AND THE LEADING BUSINESS MEN OF PERRY
Directed by Universal Producing Co.

## FREE CELEBRATION CONTESTS AT THE FAIR GROUNDS
### GATES OPEN AT NOON

**Read how to get your free ticket to the American Pioneer**—Each ticket for The American Pioneer sells for 50c and carries 10-5c coupons which will be cashed in merchandise by the leading merchants of Perry who sponsor the Business Builder Plan. Thus a full refund of the price of admission is made and The American Pioneer is furnished free to the citizens of Dallas County. **See Back page for list of merchants.**

| **50 Cents** Admits you all day and either night | Children **25c** for night sho· Free In the Afternoon |
| --- | --- |

*Promotional folder for Universal's big, experimental outdoor show, The American Pioneer, staged in Perry, Iowa. It opens to a double spread naming an extensive cast, which includes Indians, Revolutionary and Civil War soldiers, colonials, Gay Nineties characters, a ballet chorus, an international review, and Junior Uncle Sams. The back pages list supporting advertisers.*

**Touching Scene from "Corporal Eagen," Rookies Walker and Forsythe Doing "K. P."**

K-P SERVING YOUR COUNTRY ON THE POTATO PILE

This charming little scene portrays Johnston E. Walker and Dr. Forsythe peeling potatoes on "K. P. duty," just a little sideline out of the play, "Corporal Eagen, ment for South St. Paul people on two nights.

Among other features will be the singing of Jeannette Johnson in the minstrel show, which is a big part of the program, and solo

*A cartoon promotes* Corporal Eagen *in South St. Paul, Minn.*

*A* Corporal Eagan *cast at Wahoo, Nebr.*

*Poster for* The World's All Right, *the first show Fran wrote for Universal. Below are "hillbillies" and a chorus line from the production.*

Their home-talent-show years behind them, the Stewarts posed in 1948. Left to right: Raymond, Pete, sister Harriet, Merle, and Wilson.

Fran and "cast member" of her donkey baseball show.

In wartime service, Captain Franceswayne Allen of the Beech Aircraft Guardettes.

*The Franceswayne technique, demonstrated with her usual verve as she introduces home talent to a Kaiser Company cast.*

*"Take me back to Babyland. . . ." Fran as the Tell-Me-a-Story-Lady, this time with a cast of Beech Aircraft employees and their families.*

# "Take Care of Things, Will You?"

*A farm near Fairfield* became the locale for the Stewart brothers' experiment with outdoor theater. Summertime heat had always posed a problem for home talent producers. They wanted to retain their coaches and earn money year round. But before air conditioning, theaters and auditoriums could be furnace hot in the dog days, discouraging attendance. Attempting to stage shows in hot weather, which of course could not be precisely forecast, had proved unprofitable.

As the brothers cast around for a solution, they thought of all the state and county fairs crying for entertainment. They remembered that in 1929 one of their bookers, Ethel Van Hon, had arranged to have *Aunt Lucia* done in an outdoor amphitheater at Temple, Tex., attracting "people from miles around." They were aware that the Rogers Company was making a success of outdoor pageants. They were encouraged also by their new costume designer Hermine Wolff of Stuttgart, Germany, who had worked on costumes for the Passion Play in Oberammergau, Germany.

Mrs. Wolff was a valuable acquisition for the Stewarts. She had a keen eye for design and a knack for turning Stewart ideas into practical garments that the women in the costume shop could make. She knew how to make the most of available fabrics, use dyes, plan costumes to fit people of various sizes and shapes with slight adjustment, and train coaches to maintain the costumes in good condition.

Encouraged by Mrs. Wolff, the Stewarts built a semicircular stage on the farm for experiments in outdoor productions. It was 140 feet wide,

130 feet deep, and strong enough to hold not only horses but also hundreds of people. Here they tried out Mrs. Wolff's costumes against colored backdrops and developed lighting techniques using a variety of floodlights.

Their pageant *American Pioneer* premiered in Tennessee and Alabama, followed by a production in Webster City, Iowa, on June 12 and 13, 1931. Fran was allowed to help with this show, but not to direct it. That directoral plum fell to flamboyant, red-haired Elma Lightner. Fran handled publicity and promotion and familiarized herself with the show, while again billing herself as Wayne Allen of Dallas, Tex., and broadening her Missouri accent into a Texas drawl.

*American Pioneer* included scenes from United States history, from the Pilgrims' contacts with the Indians, through the embattled farmers on Concord Bridge, and up to present times. It held spots open for local events, which required that the director and/or her team had to turn playwright. At last Fran saw a possibility of getting the Stewarts to use her writing talents, but again she was disappointed. They arranged for the next pageant in Perry, Iowa, to be done by another coach.

It was not long, however, before that girl found the demands so great she went to pieces. The Stewarts wired Fran and provided her with the ticket for her first airplane ride so she could rescue the show. It was far larger than either *Aunt Lucia* or *College Flapper*. Six Universal "experts" came to handle technical matters such as the erection of the stage and installation of the microphones, loudspeakers, and lights. Wils Stewart headed the tech crew.

Fran, meanwhile, moved a step closer to her writing ambition on this assignment. A mass of historical notes had been supplied by Bessie Lyon, a teacher who was later to publish a local history. Since the material had to be reshaped for dramatic presentation, Fran wrote throughout her first night in Perry. It was a long remembered thrill.

The cast included not only more area people than she had ever used but also horses to be ridden by the Indians, the pioneers, and other historical figures. As Fran went on her search for horses and riders, the first such casting in her experience, she found that the farmers around Perry were proud of their fine animals and more than eager to show them off. She could hardly believe her good fortune in getting so many horses in the pageant.

The production was scheduled for July 4 and 5, 1931, at the fairgrounds near Perry. The premiere on July 4 was to be the truly big event. There would be a street parade at noon, followed by contests all afternoon to draw crowds. *American Pioneer* itself would climax the festivities.

Every day Fran submitted a story or stories to the paper to fan community excitement. She held a contest to select the pageant queen, Lafawn Walker, who was to ride in the big parade. Because of hard times, Fran made it possible for spectators to attend the pageant "free" by means of coupon tickets; customers paid fifty cents for the tickets, but they could redeem the attached coupons for the equivalent in merchandise at local stores. One day the paper had a whole section of stories about local history, apparently rewritten by Fran from Lyon's material to promote the coming pageant.

The main focus of her publicity was July 4. But that day it rained torrents. The whole festival had to be put off until July 5 and 6. Fran and the Stewarts had spent much more money than usual on what they thought was a sure thing. Now, when the postponed pageant opened on July 5, it was to an audience shrunken well below expectations. The resulting profit was slim.

Then another unforeseen blow fell. The farmers in the pageant decided that they should be paid for the oats their horses ate when they were serving in the cast. Oats for one horse would not have cost much, but with scores of equines involved, this meant extra expense that could run the show into the red. Such a charge had not been hinted in advance, but the farmers insisted and their mood was ugly.

The farmers had felt the Depression more severely than many other groups. They were embattled on every side by the chinch bug and other insects, drought, and ineffective governmental policies. Prices for their crops had dipped. Many were losing their farms. So whenever they saw a real or imagined injustice, they were inclined to band together and force the issue their way.

This angry militant spirit was budding in 1931. So when Franceswayne and the Stewart crew refused to accede to the farmers' demands for oats payment, groups of farmers in Indian and other costumes blocked the bridge leading from the fairgrounds into town. Since the committee and the Universal group had somehow escaped, the farm militants next surrounded the hotel where the money was being counted. They made a formidable sight; Mrs. Wolff's costumes and Fran's makeup gave them an especially fierce look.

As Wils looked out the window at the angry mob, he thought of all the things he had to do back in Fairfield. He had to get out. It was Fran, not he, who had been working with the cast anyway, so they might not recognize him if he attempted an escape. It was worth a try.

"Look, kid," he said to Fran, "you've gotten out of lots of tighter spots. I've gotta go. Take care of things, will you?" Quickly he darted away and dodged the angry riders.

Fran finished dividing the money in the usual way with her committee and secured the company's share on her person. When W.T. said to take care of things, it didn't mean to let go of the profits, of course. That was understood.

What Wilson saw as the making of a scapegoat of Fran, she saw as an advantage. She knew these Perry men as individuals. They were her friends. Furthermore, she understood farmers, since many of her relatives back in Columbia were farm people. She realized that once their mob exuberance died down, she would be able to reason with them, either if they formed a committee or spoke as individuals. All she needed to do was bide her time. That she did. The farmers paid for their own oats. She returned to Fairfield in triumph.

The company wished to continue its expansion, but the Perry experience had proved that pageants were not always sure-fire. The weather obstacle would be difficult to handle. The Stewarts decided that what they needed were better, more original plays.

Already they had employed at least one playwright, a brilliant young Parsons College student, Rex Roberts, who went on to become a Shakespearean actor, an opera performer, an author, and an engineeer. Evidently he left Universal after graduation in 1931. Now Fran was eager to take his place.

Perhaps the brothers decided they should reward her loyalty, because in the summer of 1931 Universal offered her the job as their company playwright. Even in her dreams she had asked for nothing more than this chance to prove herself. It began a new phase in Fran's career, one toward which she had been striving, hoping, and yearning.

## 21

# The
# World's All Right

*Fran made her debut* as a playwright in the autumn of 1932 when her first show was staged in Melrose Park, a Chicago suburb.

Many interruptions had delayed this event since she had received the assignment a year earlier. Her job had turned out to be as much all-purpose writer as creative playwright, engaging her in revisions of existing plays, preparing promotional material, editing the *Bulletin,* and even taking to the road to help in emergencies. Often it seemed that her titular job had to be crowded into those few odd moments she could salvage from the Stewarts' constant demands.

Not unusual in the hectic entertainment world, her show was not complete even as she waited on the station platform to entrain for Melrose Park. Raymond and Wils Stewart, still arguing over last-minute changes, had accompanied her. They paced up and down under the third-quarter moon, their breaths condensing in the late October chill.

Fran's mind was half diverted from the brothers' talk by concern over her sponsoring organization. She considered it a weak one, the Men's Club of the Evangelical Church. Most of the actors, she knew, would speak with a German accent, possibly hard to understand. In addition she faced a $150 theater rental and a 35-cent ticket charge, which made the margin for a profitable production look slim.

Fran worried, too, about the impact of the current hard times that could undercut any show. *Henry's Wedding,* with which she had served a spell in the summer just passed, had not caught on in some Minnesota towns. She had in fact flopped her first *Henry's Wedding* production, a jar-

**1 1 9**

ring experience. Other girls were meeting similar trouble making money on the road, a kind of trouble not acceptable for the Stewarts' coaches.

To help meet such problems, Universal had provided Fran with strong support for this first staging. On the platform with her were trunks containing 130 costumes, most of them of three or four pieces not counting hats. Mrs. Wolff had designed them, and the sewing shop had worked extra hard to have them ready on time. In fact, everyone at headquarters had been wonderful. She was grateful, but this added to her anxiety. The show had to make it for their sake as well as for her career.

But what were the two Stewart brothers so concerned about? Something in the show must be bothering them, but what? Raymond abruptly answered her unspoken question. "That name for your show, *American Jubilee. . . .*"

What about it?"

"It just isn't right, Allen. I don't know what it should be, but this isn't right. In fact, it stinks!" He paced angrily away, with Wils silently keeping step. Fran was shaken. A good show name was an absolute must. Even if at this late date Raymond decided *American Jubilee* stank, he must be right. In her eyes, his judgment was impeccable. Suddenly, in the midst of a stride, he wheeled around on her. "What are the opening lyrics for your first song?" he snapped.

Evidently he wanted to hear the song right on the platform. "All right, here goes." In the bright moonlight, to the tune of "Hail, Hail, the Gang's All Here," Fran sang in her off-key female baritone:

> Smile, smile, the world's all right,
> Everybody's happy, everybody's happy.
> Smile, smile, the world's all right,
> Everybody's happy now!

Jamming his right fist into his left palm, Raymond yelled, "By God, that's it. That's got it! That's got the wham! Just what we need. The name of our new show is *The World's All Right.*"

Thus on the station platform in Fairfield the name, provocative and full of promise for the show, was born. As it turned out, not only the name but the script, especially as she later revised it, turned out to be all right and then some.

Following the premiere, more and more coaches were sent out with *The World's All Right,* and happily it more than held its own with *Corporal Eagen* and *Henry's Wedding.* An *American Magazine* article in 1934 hailed it as "the company's masterpiece."

"Two hundred and twenty-five coaches are on the road, teaching the population of the United States to play parts in *The World's All Right,*" the writer reported. "The play went on the road despite all handicaps of the Depression. The script was simple, the cast long. . . . It opened with a parade of 100 tiny tots. . . . New lyrics were set to old tunes. Who did not know 'Casey Jones,' and 'Won't You Wait Till the Cows Come Home?' The town soprano sang the only difficult song, 'Kiss Me Again.' This amazing play has attracted millions of spectators and evoked the dormant histrionic ability of some of the ablest . . . businessmen in small communities."

In 1932 the public had been enchanted and obsessed with the world of radio. This extended not only to radio personalities, who received almost the same adulation as is devoted to recording and TV stars today, but to anything having to do with broadcasting. Fran, in keeping with her own developing interest in this medium, set the show in a radio studio.

The plot revolved around a young station owner, Jimmy Waddell, and his troubles with an almost defunct radio station. Advertisers who promised to hear his new program fail to appear. In the midst of his despair, who should barge in but Mr. Dinkell of Dinkell Pickles, Inc.

"Will you sign a $10,000 contract?" Wadell asks.

"I will not," Dinkell answers. "I shall go home instead and listen to the program. If it is any good, then I may sign."

At this point Fran used the device of a play within a play. The primary action occurred in the radio program, produced before a microphone with all the necessary mechanics of a radio studio. The local talent came into its glory in singing, dancing, and comedy acts. Meanwhile, the overall plot of Waddell's struggles with his financial and romantic problems (the latter centering on a girl who helped him at the station) were worked through to a happy ending. Dinkell signed the contract. The girl accepted Waddell. The show closed with a patriotic extravaganza expressing faith in America and its prosperous future.

The play's first production at Melrose Park was not identified as a premiere. In contrast to normal theater practice, Universal went to some lengths to disguise a show's premiere because sponsors wanted only successful, proven scripts. In Melrose Park, Fran used a special ploy. She showed the sponsors a fake program of a previous performance, which she had printed complete with names of the actors. These included many of her friends and relatives in Columbia and even that of her new nephew, Toby Schoyer, born the month before.

After successfully undergoing other road trials later in that fall of 1932, *The World's All Right* was judged ready for its formal premiere in Fairfield. Fairfield was the one town in the United States that saw every Universal show, and the openings there had become galas. Pictures were taken of local actors in costume, and these became part of the promotional books and press kits to be used by bookers and coaches on the road. For Fairfield the openings were a social event with all the notables and nabobs attending; it was a night to dress up, give parties, and celebrate.

Fran knew she could not get home for Christmas that year because of a stunt she was scheduled to stage for the local Rotary Club. Instead she brought her mother to Fairfield for this performance. The Stewarts entertained Ione Allen lavishly, giving a tea in her honor. Reminiscing later about this affair, Mrs. Allen recalled Wilson's wife Frances, who had gone to Stephens College in Columbia, and the Stewart half-sister Carrie (Mrs. Barns), elegant in her long velvet evening dress. Also warmly remembered were Helen Shaw, who worked in the business office, and Mrs. Wolff, who said such "lovely things" about Fran.

The Stewart guests attended the show, which proved to be a big hit, and afterward went to parties at the homes of R. R. and W. T. Stewart. The next morning Fran's mother was given a guided tour of the Universal plant, which was much larger than she had imagined, and had luncheon at the Raymond Stewarts. It was a wonderful trip for an up-to-now rather skeptical mother full of Missouri "show me" blood.

Preparing a Universal show was an elaborate process because of the two prime objectives set by the Stewarts. First the show had to be a "wham," and second, it had to be better than anything offered by the competition. What the creation of such a show involved is hinted at in a letter Fran wrote to her parents in the early spring of 1933.

"The Stewarts have set a definite schedule for me to produce so much work within a certain length of time, and I am to re-do it and put in and take out just what I think is right. When I am satisfied it is in final form, they go over it and we try it out," she wrote.

"Beginning tomorrow I am to rewrite *The World's All Right* and put more of a plot in it, which is something I have always wanted. This has to be completed by May 1st, has to be staged by June 1st, and revised and completed by June 4th when the first training class comes in. Then by the 15th of June I have to have my new show, *Crazy Politics,* written completely and then go out and stage that, so it can be revised and rewritten for the training class that comes in July 1st."

At some point in this process, Fran and Raymond and perhaps some of the others would closet themselves in an office for a think session. They would toss possible dialogue and jokes for the show back and forth or work out dance routines and song revisions, while Mary Prill or another secretary would take it all down. More than once the secretary would have to work into the early morning hours to have the script ready for them by the next day. No time must ever be lost!

There would be more than one version of the script. One would focus on dance routines and give detailed drawings and explanations. Another would contain only the play's dialogue. Separate booklets would give comic routines such as the one-minute speech, the Hill Billies, and Frankie and Johnnie.

The one-minute speech introducing *The World's All Right* ostensibly was delivered by Graham McNamee, a famous announcer of the time. It set the tone for the show, provoking waves of laughter over its topical references. The opening paragraph was a spoof of how broke everyone in the town's Depression-haunted audience felt:

> Hello everybody! What a fine crowd we have here tonight! Folks, you ought to be here with me to look into the happy smiling faces of this vast throng. And the way the crowd wear their clothes, silks, satins, ermine, diamonds, why you could buy the Empire State Building with the wealth displayed here. And all these distinguished looking gentlemen in high silk hats and full dress suits. Why every man here is in full dress suits except (local character named here), and he couldn't be because I am wearing his.

Next "McNamee" turned his satire on new inventions, current advertising promotions, and social fads:

> But I was sent out here to tell you why the world's all right. If you don't believe it is, consider our Pilgrim Fathers. They never heard of a radio whose batteries went bad, and they never had electric light and gas bills to pay on the 10th of each month. Why, folks, the world's all right. You don't realize how lucky you are. Our Pilgrim Fathers never lost money betting on major league baseball teams, and whoever heard of a Pilgrim being shot because he trumped his wife's ace at contract bridge.
>
> True, they had tobacco, but they never took the blindfold test or heard of the toasting process, and, imagine folks, the horrors of it all, no one ever told them about pink toothbrush, B.O., and halitosis. Why just look at the advantages we have today. Why, you must admit, the world's all right, or at least nowadays it smells all right.
>
> And that's not all. When our forefathers walked down the street or took a stroll in the country, about the only thing they could look at was an Indian squaw. They never had bodies by Fisher, and free wheeling was unknown.

Finally the announcer brought the audience around even to laugh at the stock market crash with this:

> And imagine living in a generation of Priscillas, John Aldens, and Miles Standishes with no Al Capone. And then think of it, they knew nothing of booms and depressions and stock market crashes. Why, heavens! When the stock market broke in those days it would mean

some peaceful cow grazing on the Boston Common had fallen down and broken her leg. But consider our stock market crash. It didn't break a cow's leg. It broke everybody.

He ended with a pep talk to put the audience in the mood for the play.

The sessions with Raymond and the others to develop such monologues, dialogues, theatrical stunts, and stage business were stimulating and creative for Fran. She enjoyed them more than anything she had yet experienced with Universal. Unfortunately, she still could not free herself from being an all-assignment promoter and troubleshooter, too. In a letter to her family she described some of these tasks:

"Mercy, I certainly am going to have to work about twelve to fourteen hours a day to put it all through on schedule. For instance tonight I will have finished ten complete merchandising plans to promote our shows, and the plans run over a six-day period. Each plan has twelve parts for each day including window displays, style shows, demonstrations, treasure hunts, and newspaper layouts. Then, two complete day-by-day procedure schedules, one for the merchandiser and the other for the girl who is to coach the show. So with the show writing added in, all in all it is a pretty big job I have staring me in the face. But I have no fear that I can't handle it. The only thing that I have to fight is the loneliness in this town." She noted that because of all the "close work," she now had to wear glasses.

Fran was still directing in the summer on a regular basis, too. During the rest of the year, she might be sent anywhere in the Midwest if there was a particularly challenging town or a crisis to be met. One such assignment occurred in Freeport, Ill., in the fall of 1933.

The coach who had started directing *The World's All Right* suddenly disappeared. She had scheduled a rehearsal at which she did not appear. The committee notified Fairfield, and Fran was dispatched. The girl's parents were called in to help find her, and the police instituted a twenty-four-hour search.

When Fran arrived, she found the coach's clothes still hanging in the hotel room. She had no inkling about how far along the missing coach was in promotion or rehearsals. Fran was in a quandary. She met resistance to her publicity, since some editors thought the company had staged the disappearance as a publicity stunt. Nevertheless, Fran somehow pulled the missing pieces together and managed to turn in a profitable cut.

As for the missing coach, a man who had picked her up while she was hitchhiking reported this to the police, and she was found with relatives in Chicago. Although she had successfully directed other plays for Universal, she confessed that the pressure had become too much and she had had to escape. Although not as mysteriously, many other girls quit for the same reason. One remembers that after several years on the road she lost her energy and inspiration and simply could not put on another show. Such work, she concluded, was only for the very young or the very strong.

Universal's office routine was no less demanding. Fran, who had often referred to herself as "horse healthy," found it necessary at times to go home to recuperate, but mostly she kept up the strenuous pace. She could do it because she loved it. She was appreciated. She was contributing. She was doing what she could do best and achieving professional status as a playwright.

Like everyone in the office she was excited that Universal was opening a New York office in the spring of 1933. "We hope to locate in the Empire State Building," she told her parents. "Really the possibilities of advancement are limitless with this organization. I think it is wonderful that I am associated with it in my own small way."

During this brief time, for Fran, the world *was* all right. In the flush of her achievements and prospects she never dreamed that she and the Stewarts would not be working together like this for years and years to come.

# ॐ 22 ॐ

# Frenetic Optimism

*If frenetic optimism* could have cured the Depression, it would have been short-lived indeed. Politicians, businesspeople, and editors all pounded the theme that the Depression was on its way out. Well in the vanguard of these cheerful propagandists was Universal.

The company's promotions strained to out-Barnum Barnum. If the reader could be conveyed backward in time to a small town on a Saturday evening in September 1933, he or she would have witnessed a prime example. Down Fourth, Liberty, Third, and Washington streets, all lined with spectators, wound a parade.

First came the police escort. Then the Elks Club's drum and bugle corps and the Boy Scouts, followed by floats constructed and decorated by local business firms, a new Packard, a new Studebaker roadster, an old Ford, a horse and buggy, and other cars and trucks including the Budweiser Brewery truck from which an old-fashioned German band blared loudly. Signs and banners festooned the vehicles; they hung from radiator caps, the backs of cars, and down the backs of the band players. A flickering glow was cast over the scene by torches improvised from broomstick handles wound with old rags and dipped in kerosene.

Perched on fenders, in trucks, on floats, and in open cars were costumed entertainers, passing or throwing out handbills. One truck carried a screaming load of children with banners identifying them as the Sophisticated Kiddies with their Nifty Nursemaids. The local patrol wagon held two gangsters types who were constantly being nabbed and renabbed in a moving pantomime by the police. Two women sang in high soprano:

> We're Women Walter Winchells
> We've got a nose for news
> Since women folks have got the vote
> This world has changed its views.
> In Centerville, so we've been told
> There are rumors everywhere
> That the women all will rally
> To elect a woman mayor.

Riding in the car of honor was the female candidate, dolled up with a parasol and puffing on a cigar. The crowd hardly had an opportunity to wonder at this before two carloads of politicians went by chorusing to the tune of "Shuffle Off to Buffalo":

> You can bet your bottom dollar
> That we have no cause to holler
> Things are all okay
> Hey, Hey, Hey!
> And we're glad we're living
> In the good old U.S.A.
> Take the map and choose a state
> Any one of forty-eight
> And move in today,
> Hey, Hey, Hey!
> You'll be glad you're living
> In the good old U.S.A.

A loudspeaker spouted political announcements, adding to the bedlam.

Masterminding the whole hoopla was Franceswayne. She had met the paraders at the Elks Club headquarters with hammer, tacks, pins, twine, scissors, and crepe paper to be cut into streamers. With experience dating back to childhood when she had preened as a fairy queen on her father's piano-truck float in Columbia parades, she had made up this moving exhibition just as she would have a show cast. She sent them on their way shortly after eight that evening with the instructions, "Come on, everyone, smile. Wave to the people. Make lots of noise. And smile."

The town was not as the lyrics indicated, Centerville; it was Winona, Minn. Nor was the cigar-puffing lady in the open car really running for mayor. Yet interest in the parade had built beyond normal heights because this *was* an election week in Winona. Further, it was an election that had stirred emotions more deeply (not only in Winona but nation-wide) than almost any held in America, for at issue was the repeal of Prohibition. Factions on both sides, with their posters and slogans, marched in Fran's parade, adding to the excitement.

Obviously the parade had not been organized to publicize the real election. It was part of the promotion for Fran's new play, *Crazy Politics,* which was to be staged in Winona the following week starting on Election day September 12, 1933, and also running the next evening.

This show outdid the rampant optimism of *The World's All Right* with its sometimes forced good cheer. And with the lucky conjunction of the real election and Fran's parade and publicity, *Crazy Politics* scored a smash hit in Winona. Its success was particularly welcome, for Universal's profits had begun to decline in 1933. The Stewarts' answer, like that of all good fighters, had been to struggle all the harder. *Crazy Politics* was one weapon.

The brothers showed no lack of courage in meeting the Depression head-on. Their strategy was to pour pep, enthusiasm, and hard work into selling more and expanding. Such optimism worked at first. The bookers signed up so many Universal plays in both the United States and Canada that coaches could be sent out all that summer of 1933. Despite the *American Pioneer* fiasco, the company now provided both indoor and outdoor summer contracts. If the sponsoring group chose the outdoors, Universal would furnish the know-how as well as specialized lighting equipment.

That summer, Universal opened its New York office, not in the Empire State Building, but at 580 Fifth Avenue, close enough to Radio City Music Hall so that Merle Stewart could look out his office window and see the Rockettes practicing on a nearby roof.

That branch office would profit the company for the next two years with Merle as its manager and coach Mary Crowley as its assistant manager. They would hire, train, and supervise coaches in the area, and Mary would publish an East Coast version of the coaches' *Bulletin*. Temporary branches, mostly for training coaches or bookers, were advertised as being located in other cities, including Princeton, N.J., Cleveland, Atlanta, Minneapolis, Boston, and Chicago.

At headquarters Fran kept busy on show revisions. She updated *Henry's Wedding* and called it *In the Money*. She changed the gangsters of the first show to fake rajahs in the second. The explosion scene was replaced, making it easier to recruit actors for that somewhat frightening stunt. A new finale pounded in the spirit of optimism to the tune of "Happy Days Are Here Again." It ran:

> Wedding bells are ringing out
> The whole world seems to dance and shout!
> Let's dance a dance
> And turn about.
> Wedding bells are ringing out!
>
> A happy bride and a happy groom;
> There's no reason to think of gloom,

> The whole world seems to be in tune.
> Wedding bells are ringing out!

In March 1934 Fran premiered another play, *Take It Easy,* in Fairfield. This play started with a minstrel, including an Interlocutor and Bones exchanging jokes and introducing various singing and dancing choruses, a new way to start a Universal show.

*Take It Easy* dealt with the backstage life of show people who were trying to stage a Broadway play. They were in trouble unless Fritzie, the leading lady, was willing to marry the show's rich backer. Fritzie, of course, had other ideas, for she was in love with a young bridge builder from South America. Several characters seemed patterned on Universal Producing company personnel, namely the chief costumer, Hermine Wolff, and three of the Stewarts.

Later in 1934 the Stewarts scored a publicity goal not achieved by any other producing company in that decade. They became the subject of national publicity in the *American Magazine.* The article began:

> Like to go on the stage? Here's how 300,000 folks are getting their chance. Stars of the cast are village doctors, merchants, fire chiefs, mayors. Every night is amateur night in more than 60 American communities, hometown theatricals in mass production.

The *American* writer went on to describe how Universal shows were sold, how casts were recruited, and what the productions were like.

Much of the copy was devoted to a laudatory interview with Raymond Stewart, but the article also told of the history of the company, its seven successful plays and particularly, as previously noted, *The World's All Right.* It described what the coach did and the good feelings that home talent productions created in a town. Certainly the *American Magazine* piece should have given a substantial boost to Universal.

Nonetheless, as 1934 wore on, cracks had begun to appear in even the determinedly optimistic picture projected by the Stewarts. For one thing, Universal was now *the* company to beat, and its rivals, both great and small, were competing more effectively. They hired away Universal coaches and bookers to learn the Stewarts' secrets, thus eliminating earlier Stewart advantages. Some tried underhand means to destroy Universal. Coach Marie Ferguson wrote the brothers of one such incident in late 1934.

A stranger came to her rehearsal claiming to be a Universal booker. After she had welcomed him, he launched into a diatribe before the entire cast "about what a rotten company we are. He said some pretty raw things." Thinking fast, she told him plainly that the Stewarts "couldn't be expected to tolerate drinkers on our staff." He wasn't drunk, but that made the people think he was, so he was ordered out. "Luckily the group's attitude was one of profound sympathy for me."

Another problem, already evident in 1933, grew to alarming proportions in the following year. Expenses often outweighed profits. In some states, coaches now had to hire professional stagehands and pay union wages. Grace Barrington remembers that during a first rehearsal she found the piano had to be moved. Cast members refused to help, and she had to hire two stagehands for twenty-five dollars, a huge sum in those days.

Advertising costs climbed. When the company tried to overcome this by hiring a single printer to produce the illustrated broadsheets and handbills, he ran too late to service the first shows of the season. Meanwhile, Universal had invested in costly, handsomely bound advertising books for all the coaches. Another new expense was the lighting equipment for the summer shows. The branch offices began to exert a financial drain.

Then came the terrible 1934 drought, which turned much of the Midwest into the fearsome Dust Bowl destroying communities, lifetime savings, and the hopes for the future of thousands and thousands in a manner more damaging than the Depression itself. Neither high-powered promotion nor hyped-up optimism could make much headway against the Dust Bowl. Bookings nose-dived; Universal shows either were canceled or failed. In addition, Orville Prill recalls that Canadian authorities closed the border to Universal shows in order to stem the southward flow of Canadian money. In the face of these setbacks, the forward momentum of the company had slowed seriously by the end of 1934.

In addition to company troubles, the end of that year was a particularly sad time for Fran. In September her mother died. Although never quite as close to her mother as to her father, in later years their relationship had become increasingly important and warm because of Ione's encouragement for Fran's career. Now this firm, loving support was gone.

Then there was the *American Magazine* article. Ever since it had appeared Fran had been nursing a heartache. Sure, it had been good for the company. Sure, it had pleased the Stewarts. But its effect on Fran had been destructive. She had thought that she had forged a strong relationship with the brothers, that she had become one of their team, and that they appreciated her as much as she admired them. The article seemed to indicate how wrong she had been.

With all its praise for *The World's All Right,* Fran had neither been named as its author nor in any other way. Even worse than no mention at all was the paragraph devoted to writing. It stated that Raymond "likes to write dialogue but not plays," and continued in words that stamped themselves on her brain:

> To give himself more time to train salesmen and supervise the business Raymond Stewart employed a playwright, a university girl, just as he would employ a stenographer, and assigned her to a studio to hammer out vehicles for the nation's amateur talent.

So that was how the Stewarts really regarded her, "a university girl?" That was long past. Since then she had become one of their top dramatic directors, top coaching teacher, top promoter, and now their playwright and minor executive. Or so she had thought. Despite all the surface camaraderie and their acknowledgement of her authorship of *Crazy Politics* when it premiered in Fairfield, they must feel they could hire almost anyone off the street to replace her.

Wasn't that attitude also reflected in the compensation they gave her—$110 per month? While this was by no means a rock-bottom wage for the Depression, still it seemed inadequate in the light of her contributions to the company. She wanted very much to go home for Christmas, especially since it would be her father's first alone. However, as usual, most of her salary was already committed, and she could not afford to give up a week's pay. Neither paid vacations nor any other fringes were offered by Universal. Christmas at home had to be forfeited.

A different kind of project soon came to Fran's desk and helped revive her spirits. She began working with the brothers on a biblical pageant. It was called *The First Commandment* and grouped several Bible stories. With their religious upbringing, the Stewarts were well qualified to contribute to this theme. It represented, however, an abrupt about-face from their earlier frenetic optimism, now rendered obsolete by the Dust Bowl and the deep Depression. Instead, *The First Commandment* was intended to promote reverence and a turning to the Almighty for succor.

Before the pageant was far along, however, the Stewarts sent Fran to Cedar Rapids, Iowa, to stage an especially demanding production of *The World's All Right.* By then she was having serious thoughts of leaving Universal for good. So, whether to free herself from debt so she could leave or as a last effort to impress the Stewarts, there was something almost desperate in how she publicized the show.

Daily she barraged the paper with interesting and chatty stories. There were writeups about the backgrounds of individual actors, about the Coe College Physical Education Department girls who would dress in "high-brown makeup and gay calico costumes" for the Darktown Strutters Chorus, and about the high school girls and the numbers they would do. There were stories about the hillbilly comic routine and the hillbilly band, about the show's Frankie and Johnny number, which featured "Dean Stauffacher in peroxide curls and Ervin Stepanek in waxed moustache." She wrote about the specially vested choir, including choir members from various Cedar Rapids churches, and about a reading to be done by the Reverend J. Renwick McCullough, pastor of Westminster Presbyterian Church. There were descriptions of the parts to be played by the uniformed United States Naval Communications Reserve and the drum and bugle corps of the American Legion.

Since many Bohemians lived in Cedar Rapids, she publicized the performance of the Beseda, the Czech national dance, using "genuine festive attire, ornate and beautiful." Four hundred local people would take part in the show, the newspapers reported, and it would be staged at the Memorial Coliseum to allow seating for all their relatives and friends. As a final assurance that the whole town would know about the show, Fran advertised it in a lavish, movie-type ad. The crowds flocked in, and she made a handsome profit.

Back in Fairfield she worked harder than ever through March. She paid her debts and held onto some money. After collecting her March salary, she went home to Columbia.

Fran told Universal her trip was for a rest and vacation and at first made no firm decision. Yet the longer she stayed, and the more she talked with her father about her future prospects, the less attractive a return to Fairfield seemed. The company might or might not recover from the severe setbacks it had experienced. She had produced enough scripts to last for several years, and the Stewarts would not need her as a playwright. To return would mean a disheartening demotion back to full-time coaching on the road along with the many directors she had trained.

At home Fran learned that a friend of hers, Lucille Elwood, was now working for Ingram Producing Company, based in Rock Island, Ill. She wrote Lucille and was invited to come to work for Ingram. On July 7, 1935, she arrived in Rock Island, ending her seven-year association with Universal Producing Company.

Those Universal years had been constructive, exciting ones. The professional expertise as a show director, promoter, and playwright that Fran acquired with the Stewarts were to stand her in good stead for the rest of her life. With a loyalty that disregarded its lukewarm reciprocation, she always looked back with gratitude for all she had learned from the brothers.

Fran and the Stewarts were flint and steel. The brothers, hard-headed, of good judgment, straitlaced, money-oriented, and imaginative planners were single-mindedly devoted to business success. Fran, talented, loyal, courageous to the point of recklessness, pleasure and people loving, and careless of money and the morrow, too often wore her heart on her sleeve. Yet when the flint and steel struck sparks at Universal they made home talent's greatest team of the 1928–35 era.

# POSTSCRIPT

*After parting company* the Stewarts and Franceswayne followed contrary destinies.

The Stewarts lost other key people during the Depression doldrums and never recovered the momentum or earnings they had enjoyed when Fran and the other professionals were on the road or in the office. Their new show, *The First Commandment,* which the Stewarts completed after Fran started it, flopped on the road despite lavish costuming. Rewrites of Fran's radio-theme shows, culminating in *The Radio Festival of 1937,* had only mediocre success.

A crippling blow fell when Universal's costumes were destroyed in a fire. Innovatively, the Stewarts fought back by staging home talent contests along the lines of those popularized by Major Bowes on radio, in which the contestants furnished their own get-ups. Promotion for these shows featured simulated interviews with people in downtown areas, giving them the thrill of talking over that symbol of radio glamour, the microphone.

Next the brothers turned to renting movies and showing them in towns that had no movie houses. In several Iowa towns they even built their own theaters. They distributed films for school assemblies, one ill-fated example being Hitler's *Mein Kampf.* Yet prosperity continued to elude them.

In 1940 they turned to their long-idle costume sewing machines. Initial success came with a contract to supply Montgomery Ward a muslin liner for a baby basket. Another type of liner followed with a contract to supply the Woolworth chain. They added closet accessories to their lines. Now that the Stewarts were prospering in the manufacturing business, all theater-related projects were abandoned.

The brothers throve, put on weight, and lived the rest of their lives mainly in Fairfield as successful manufacturers. Dynamic Wilson T. Stewart was the first to die in 1960 at the age of 55. The surviving brothers sold the firm in 1967 to the Perfect Film and Chemical Company of Manhasset, N.Y. Raymond died in 1968, Weston in 1976, and Merle in 1978.

The Stewarts' home talent operation left America a manifold inheritance, which ranged from church steeples to park benches to American Legion kitchens to school pianos and scores of other civic improvements that their shows helped finance. Universal home talent income benefited countless needy children, unemployed persons, and inmates of hospitals and old people's homes.

Perhaps Universal's greatest legacy was the training it provided its elite corps of dramatic directors, which superbly equipped them for constructive roles in community and business affairs. These young women went on to manage companies, become journalists and authors, and head political and civic organizations in addition to roles as homemakers and mothers.

Alone of this group, Franceswayne Allen made home talent her lifelong career. Separated from Universal in 1935, she had no easier time at first than did her erstwhile employers. She had a fling with Ingram Producing Company of Rock Island, Ill., and another doing home talent contests as a means of finding performers for the WLS Radio Station Barn Dance in Chicago. In 1937 she returned to Columbia, Mo., where she became a radio announcer for the home talent Ozark Openhouse on station KFRU and did live versions of the show in the Columbia listening area. She also had several radio programs and made personal appearances as Susie Q. Sizzle, the Streamlined Hillbilly.

In 1940 she and her father collaborated in writing two home talent productions, *Funzapoppin'* and *Hayloft Festival,* which they took on the road under the auspices of radio station KIBW, Topeka, Kans. With the advent of World War II, Fran was hired as a Guardette at Beech Aircraft Corporation in Wichita, Kans. There she put on in-plant versions of home talent shows as morale builders. After the war she married Hugh Blair "Buck" Cochran, and in partnership with her husband and father, wrote and staged *Fun for You.*

A decisive turn in her career came shortly afterward when she joined Empire Producing Company of Kansas City, Mo. Its president, George De Haven, had greeted her in their first meeting as "a legend in her time," and she had recognized in him a "terrifically promotion-minded executive." They teamed up with the aim of making home talent history. On her first show for Empire in Lewiston, Idaho, Fran grossed $3,084, one of the largest returns of her career. By the 1950s Empire was staging 2,300 shows annually, possibly a record for any producer.

An even greater plus for Fran was her association with De Haven. He embodied for her all the Stewarts had been and much they failed to be. More appreciative, more sympathetic, more generous in times of difficulty, he proved a loyal friend. Fran became Empire's playwright, turning out a show about every eight months, for a total of thirteen. She also assisted in management, trained coaches, and went on the road herself.

The apex of her directing experience came in industrial recreation shows. Here, "the show is not the ultimate goal," Fran noted, "but rather the play that goes into creating it . . . and shapes that intangible *esprit de corps* which big business feels is invaluable." She directed shows for Kaiser Industries twice, Texas Instruments, and John Hancock Life Insurance Company. She hugely enjoyed the companies' red carpet treatment of her, the union stage crews, professional orchestras, and quality wardrobes. But such shows proved to be a fad that soon vanished.

On another home talent frontier in 1958, Fran invaded Alaska where she staged shows in the principal cities with considerable success. But already home talent, as Fran had known it, was doomed by the ballooning popularity of TV. As the 1960s began, the "one-eyed monster" had preempted the hometown amusement audience. Public interest in home talent plummeted. Empire, like Universal, was forced into other lines of business.

Fran's outlook grew bleak. Her husband Buck had died in 1952, her father in 1955. She had no savings. For most of her career she had money only if a show made it. She always counted on the next production to keep her going. Now there was no next. De Haven offered her a job managing an apartment building in which he had an interest in Dallas, Tex. There she continued for a year or so until falling ill.

She went to Pittsburgh to live with her sister while recovering. Her Pittsburgh physician advised against telling her that her illness was diagnosed as cancer. Although growing progressively weaker, nothing could diminish her enthusiasm for home talent shows and her determination to continue working with them in some capacity.

She liked to reminisce with the family about how she had done it all, from Chautauqua performances to Tom Thumb weddings, minstrels, musical comedies, hillbilly shows, outdoor pageants, amateur contests, and even donkey baseball and talent scouting.

Her nephews were awed that she had played in every state in the Union with the exception of Hawaii and in all but one Canadian province. She had worked with every type of civic organization. She estimated she had conducted shows in at least 500 towns. Average cast size was 125, bringing the total she had directed to 62,500. Average attendance for a two-night stand was 900. She had trained hundreds of directors.

Early in June 1965 her sister brought her a letter from a friend in the Empire organization. The writer expressed the well-meaning hope that, now that Fran could no longer continue in show business, she would make permanent living arrangements in Pittsburgh. Suddenly it was as though a door had been slammed and locked against her. Three days later she was dead.

Fran Allen's life expressed the integrity of devotion to one career and making the most she could of it. Home talent was the be-all and end-all for which she journeyed across all the stars in the flag. Each town in which she halted became her hearthstone where she assembled a family for the duration. The older members of the cast were her brothers, sisters, uncles, aunts, parents, and grandparents; the young people, the children she never had. Her unusual name, Franceswayne, occasionally turns up among their descendants.

She left her body to the Pittsburgh Medical Center for cancer research. After her memorial service in Calvary Episcopal Church, Pittsburgh, a friend offered a tribute she would have liked. "She's just gone on to the only new territory she could play," he said. "And if I know Fran, she's already got St. Peter signed up for the Flapper Chorus."

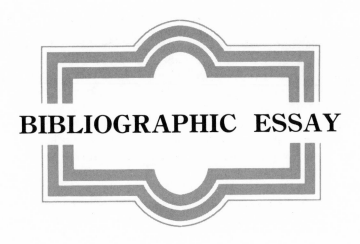

# BIBLIOGRAPHIC ESSAY

THANK HEAVEN for dedicated correspondents, for without the records they leave, much history would never be written. During the long, lonely evenings in the small towns where Franceswayne Allen coached, she described her experiences in detailed letters (some running over twenty pages) that she sent to her father, her sister, and others. Training at the University of Missouri Journalism School and subsequent news experience sharpened her naturally keen power of observation and her ear for dialogue. In Fran's narratives, color, action, and speech spring from the page.

Her accounts focused on her adventures as a show director and playwright for Universal Producing Company. They were the core for this book. Notable among this material were twenty-five single-spaced typewritten pages narrating her triumphs and mishaps in twenty-seven towns, probably a rewriting of letters to her father and intended for the book she planned. Much of this has been used verbatim. The training class chapters were largely re-created from a series of letters to her father, which he kept in her old doll trunk. In a 1962 letter to Raymond Stewart, Fran reminisced about Universal events, including the naming and launching of their most successful show, and traced her later career.

A short story attempt by Fran provided the chapter "Getting His Teeth into the Act." Her extensive collection of other memorabilia—show programs and schedules, handwritten notes, lists of towns visited, fliers, promotional material, photographs, clippings, and the like—provided insight into Fran's character.

Copies of the *Bulletin,* a Universal publication for their coaches, were loaned to Dr. Eckey by Helen (Mrs. Weston) Stewart. They provided additional data on Fran and other coaches, including the towns they played, their earnings, and their contest rankings. The *Bulletin* revealed the chronology of Fran's shows and made it possible to locate publicity in newspaper files in forty-six towns. This often provided additional data about shows and surrounding circumstances as well as corroborating Fran's account.

In developing the Universal story, the personal reminiscences of Merle and Helen Stewart, Orville and Mary Prill, and others associated with the company were key sources. Further, besides the *Bulletin,* the Stewarts loaned the authors an extensive array of scripts, promotional brochures, clippings, directives, manuals used by bookers and coaches, and coaches' daily procedures. Another valuable source on booking practices was the late Ethel Van Hon.

A wealth of information about the four Stewart brothers and Universal came from the *Fairfield Ledger,* covering many years of the Stewarts' careers there. The Fairfield Public Library contributed valuable additional material, including show broadsheets. The Museum of Repertoire Americana, Mt. Pleasant, Iowa, provided the script for *Corporal Eagen.*

Further light was thrown on the Universal scene by some of the about 1,000 women and several men who were Universal coaches. Dr. Eckey interviewed fourteen of these and an additional thirty-two coaches responded in writing. One key document, the script of *Aunt Lucia,* was furnished by Thelma Bump. Others loaned newspaper clippings, handbills, pictures, and other memorabilia. The most valuable contributions were personal reminiscences (many on cassette tapes) that came from twenty-five coaches, helping recreate the excitement, struggles, and nearly unbelievable accomplishments of these talented young "pilgrims of the impossible."

Since Universal was not an isolated phenomenon, we sought to picture the company within the context of an American theatrical development. Major contributions were made by Jerome H. Cargill and George De Haven. Other sources included William E. Munsey and the late William W. Munsey, as well as others of the John B. Rogers Producing Company; Marjorie Dunaway Hatchett of the Wayne P. Sewell Producing Company; and others associated with organizations competing in the intense rivalry that permeated the home talent field.

Two books added glimpses of home talent as viewed by the public: Harlow R. Hoyt's *Town Hall Tonight* (New York: Prentice-Hall, Inc., 1955), and MacKinlay Kantor's *But Look, the Morn: The Story of a Childhood* (New York: Coward-McCann, 1947). Each tells of its author's boyhood participation in such shows. An insider's view is offered by Minnie Pearl with Joan Dew in *Minnie Pearl: An Autobiography* (New York: Simon and Schuster, 1980), which includes several chapters on her experiences with the Wayne P. Sewell Producing Company.

Over a half century a handful of magazines explored the home talent phenomenon. Some of them were the *American Magazine,* with its article on Universal in the November, 1934 issue, *The Saturday Evening Post, The Billboard, Liberty, The Newnan Times-Herald Centennial Magazine, Coronet, Pathfinder,* and *The Kiwanis Magazine.* Most of the articles were publicity, inspired by one or another producer, but they did clarify the state and extent of the home talent movement at the time of their publication.

In the Grinberg Library, New York City, Dr. Eckey viewed a filmstrip showing a costumed Flapper Chorus in performance in a production of *Aunt Lucia* staged by Grace Barrington in Alameda, Calif. (Paramount Newsreel sound film #894, issue 52, 1931). It is the only video record of this famous act of which the authors are aware.

Dr. Eckey traveled to towns and cities in thirteen states and wrote over a hundred letters of inquiry to gather material. She was met with interest, kindness, and helpfulness everywhere. To all these contributors go sincere thanks for helping to rescue from obscurity the vibrant theater that once played on 1,001 hometown Broadways.

# INDEX